Given by
Sherry Parrish
April 2011

Resist! 2011

~~Counts as a book social action~~

DATE DUE		
D. Dennis		8-14-11

Also by Michael G. Long

The Legacy of Billy Graham: Critical Reflections on America's Greatest Evangelist

First Class Citizenship: The Civil Rights Letters of Jackie Robinson

God and Country: Diverse Perspectives on Christianity and Patriotism (with Tracy Wenger Sadd)

Billy Graham and the Beloved Community: America's Evangelist and the Dream of Martin Luther King Jr.

Martin Luther King Jr. on Creative Living

Against Us, but for Us: Martin Luther King Jr. and the State

RESIST!

Christian Dissent for the 21st Century

Michael G. Long, Editor

ORBIS BOOKS

Maryknoll, New York 10545

Copyright © 2008 by Michael G. Long.
Published by Orbis Books, Maryknoll, NY 10545–0308.
All rights reserved.

Portions of the chapter by Jack Nelson-Pallmeyer, "Resisting Violence, Creating Peace," appeared in different form in Jack Nelson-Pallmeyer and Bret Hesla, *Worship in the Spirit of Jesus: Theology, Liturgy, and Songs without Violence*, pp. 53–57. Copyright © 2005 The Pilgrim Press. Reference used by permission.

Queries regarding rights and permissions should be addressed to: Orbis Books, P.O. Box 308, Maryknoll, NY 10545–0308.

Manufactured in the United States of America.
Manuscript editing and typesetting by Joan Weber Laflamme.

Library of Congress Cataloging-in-Publication Data

Resist! : Christian dissent for the 21st century / edited by Michael G. Long.
    p. cm.
    ISBN 978–1–57075–800–3
  1. Christianity and justice. I. Long, Michael G.
    BR115.J8R47 2008
    261.8—dc22

2008020080

For James H. Zeisloft,
faithful preacher of Christian resistance

Contents

PART 3
ORDINARY CHRISTIANS,
EXTRAORDINARY HOPE

Acknowledgments

Countless signs point to the urgent need for Christian resistance in the twenty-first century. One of these signs, however minor, is the overwhelmingly positive response that I received when I began to recruit first-rank scholars, university chaplains, and activists to contribute to this volume. Their easy willingness, their encouraging words, and their exceptional contributions have made this project one of the more rewarding experiences of my professional career, and I thank my colleagues for sharing their creative expertise so that the rest of us can think and act more faithfully as we become Christian resisters throughout the world.

I offer my immediate thanks, too, to Robert Ellsberg, publisher and editor-in-chief at Orbis Books, whose career truly embodies the best of Christian resistance. With his steady guidance, Orbis has become a reliable beacon of hope for Christians seeking to make a way out of no way. The contributors and I could not be more pleased than we are that *Resist!* is in his hands.

Sharon Herr has once again proven to be the most capable of proofreaders, and I continue to be immensely grateful for her red pen, but even more, for her priceless friendship. Sharon and I have been friends for more than a decade now, and there are few things I hope for more fervently than the opportunity to enjoy her company for decades to come.

Jeff Long, a scholar of Hinduism with an international reputation, chairs the department of religious studies at our home institution, Elizabethtown College in Pennsylvania, and my gratitude runs deep for his collegial spirit and enthusiastic support for my scholarship. My gratitude also extends to my stunning students, all of them undergraduates, who inspire me in surprising ways. If I have a bit of a rebellious spirit in me, it is largely because of my weekly encounters with their youthful rants against "the system."

And if I have a bit of idealism in me, it is mostly because of my daily encounters with our two sons, Jackson Griffith and Nathaniel Finn, resisters *extraordinaire*. Their smiles and tears, their dreams and nightmares, their hopes and fears are reason enough for me to believe through disbelief that the world, with our help, will one day become "the beloved community" that Martin Luther King Jr. dreamed of for his own family.

Thanks upon thanks to Karin, Jack, and Nate.

Contributors

Jeff Bach, Director of the Young Center for Anabaptist and Pietist Studies at Elizabethtown College, is an ordained minister in the Church of the Brethren and the author of the award-winning *Voices of the Turtledoves: The Sacred World of Ephrata.*

Deborah K. Blanks is Associate Dean of Religious Life and the Chapel at Princeton University. She is an ordained minister in the African Methodist Episcopal Church and a contributor to *This Is My Story: Testimonies and Sermons of Black Women in Ministry.*

Alison L. Boden, Dean of Religious Life and the Chapel at Princeton University, has written extensively on religion and social justice. Her most recent book is *Women's Rights and Religious Practice: Claims in Conflict.*

Paula M. Cooey serves as the Margaret W. Harmon Professor of Theology and Culture at Macalester College. She has published several books on Christian theology and ethics, including *Willing the Good: Jesus, Dissent, and Desire.*

Curtiss Paul DeYoung, Professor of Reconciliation Studies at Bethel University, is a leading authority on Christian reconciliation and has just authored *Living Faith: How Faith Inspires Social Justice.*

Roberto S. Goizueta, Professor of Theology at Boston College, has written extensively on Hispanic Christian theology, including *Caminenos con Jesús: Toward a Hispanic/Latino Theology of Accompaniment.* He has recently co-edited *Hispanic Christian Thought at the Dawn of the Twenty-First Century: Apuntes in Honor of Justo L. Gonzales.*

Stanley Hauerwas is the Gilbert T. Rowe Professor of Theological Ethics at Duke University. He has authored many books and articles on Christian social ethics, and his most recent publication is *Matthew,* a biblical commentary.

Dwight N. Hopkins, Professor of Theology in the Divinity School at the University of Chicago, has authored and edited numerous studies in black Christian theology, including *Introducing Black Theology of Liberation.* One of his most recent books is *Being Human: Race, Culture, and Religion.*

Dolores R. Leckey, Senior Research Fellow at the Woodstock Theological Center of Georgetown University, has written on Christian spirituality and the Catholic laity. Her most recent book is *The Laity and Christian Education: Apostolicam Actuositatem, Gravissimum Educationis.*

Bill McKibben is a world-renowned environmentalist whose bestselling books include *Deep Economy: The Wealth of Communities and the Durable Future.* He is an active member of the United Methodist Church and a scholar-in-residence at Middlebury College.

William L. (Scotty) McLennan is Dean for Religious Life as well as Lecturer in Political Economy at Stanford University. He is also co-author of *Church on Sunday, Work on Monday: The Challenge of Fusing Christian Values with Business Life.*

Jack Nelson-Pallmeyer is Associate Professor of Justice and Peace Studies at the University of St. Thomas. His numerous books on religion and social ethics include *Is Religion Killing Us? Violence in the Bible and the Quran.*

Larry L. Rasmussen, Reinhold Niebuhr Professor Emeritus of Social Ethics at Union Theological Seminary of New York City, has authored or edited many books in Christian environmental ethics and Christian political thought, including *Earth Community Earth Ethics* (winner of the Louisville Grawemeyer Award) and *Dietrich Bonhoeffer: Reality and Resistance.*

Paul Raushenbush is Associate Dean of Religious Life and the Chapel at Princeton University. A contributing editor for Beliefnet.com, he is also the editor of *Christianity and the Social Crisis in the Twenty-First Century: The Classic That Woke Up the Church.*

Tracy Wenger Sadd serves as Chaplain and Director of Religious Life, as well as Lecturer in Religion, at Elizabethtown College. She is the author of several books and is co-editor of *God and Country? Diverse Perspectives on Christianity and Patriotism.*

Christine M. Smith, Professor of Preaching at the United Theological Seminary of the Twin Cities, is an expert on preaching justice and the author of several books, including *Preaching as Weeping, Confession, and Resistance: Radical Responses to Radical Evil.*

Douglas Sturm is Professor Emeritus of Religion and Political Science at Bucknell University. He is the author of many works on religion and politics, including *Belonging Together: Faith and Politics in a Relational World.*

Valerie Weaver-Zercher is a writer, editor, and mother in Mechanicsburg, Pennsylvania. Her feature articles, essays, book reviews, and poetry have appeared in *Sojourners*, *Christian Century*, *Books and Culture*, *Brain*, *Child*, and *The Mennonite*, and a chapter of hers appears in *The Maternal Is Political: Women Writers at the Intersection of Motherhood and Social Change*.

Samuel Wells, Dean of the Chapel and Research Professor of Christian Ethics at Duke University, has written five books on Christian theology and ethics, including *Power and Passion: Six Characters in Search of Resurrection*.

Introduction

Christianity Is Resistance

Michael G. Long

MY COUNTRY, RIGHT OR WRONG

"Christianity breeds patriotism."[1] This is the statement that Billy Graham made when reflecting on the thousands of young men and women, many of them Christian pacifists, who resisted the Vietnam War in 1965. For the evangelist, Christians who protested the war, and especially those who practiced civil disobedience, simply failed to be true to their faith—a faith that instructs the followers of Jesus not to resist but to support and honor the governing authorities. Resistance is for wild-eyed, long-haired, pot-smoking radicals, not for God-fearing Christians.

Unsurprisingly, Graham abided by his own counsel, and in 1965 he sent an encouraging letter to President Lyndon Johnson. "You are getting some unjust criticism," he wrote, "but remember that the most criticized men in America were those whose names shine brightest in human history. . . . Also, remember they crucified Jesus within three years after he began his public ministry."[2]

Contrary to Johnson's critics, Graham believed that the Vietnam War was a holy war against godless communists intent on the wholesale destruction of Christian civilization, and few things sickened him more than the sight of young Christian men burning their draft cards and resisting the war raging in Vietnam.[3] When asked in 1968 whether he would counsel a young man to support the war effort, Graham stated: "Well, I think that when our nation makes a commitment, right or wrong, I have a responsibility to my nation. . . . I think when we are called upon, we have to serve."[4]

MAY WE RESIST?
REMEMBERING OUR ANCESTORS

Graham's stance during the Vietnam War raises an important question for Christians as we begin to make our way through this shockingly violent century: May we resist our governing authorities? If we disagree with our leaders—if we find their execution of the current war in Iraq to be as unjust and immoral as the Vietnam War turned out to be, or if we believe their economic policies reflect a preferential option for the rich rather than for the poor, or if we are convinced that they are idolatrous when they prescribe that we stand up and place our hand over our hearts as the national anthem plays, or if we discover their environmental policies contribute to the destruction of our planet—may we, as Christians, resist the powers that be? Or must we assume the role of good patriots who support our country and its leaders, right or wrong? In other words, does our faith really breed an uncritical patriotism?

Of course not—Christianity *is* resistance.

It's resistance to a politics that, among other things, kills the people of God. Let's go back to our origins, not to the rise of flag-waving Christianity in the United States, but to two of our early faith ancestors—Shiphrah and Puah.[5] Although largely unknown to folks in the pew, these two courageous Hebrew midwives offer a significant clue about the essential character of our faith.

Here's their story from the Book of Exodus: Shiphrah and Puah received a direct order from the king of Egypt to kill any and all male babies born to Hebrew women—an order that reflected the pharaoh's paranoid belief that the growth of the Hebrew population posed an imminent threat to the vital interests of Egypt and that killing off innocent baby boys would solve the problem.

But there was one thing the great pharaoh could not control—the virulent strain of political resistance in the Hebrew faith of these two midwives. Although the consequences of disobeying the mighty pharaoh could have been deadly, Shiphrah and Puah did not throw their hands up and say "our leader, right or wrong." Instead, these courageous women focused on the real and present danger that the pharaoh posed to their own faith, to their abiding belief that God willed the liberation of the Hebrew people. And so, rather than murdering the baby boys, Shiphrah and Puah "feared God; they did not do as the king of Egypt commanded them; but they let the boys live" (Ex 1:17).

The story of Shiphrah and Puah is just one of the many stories of courageous resistance that are available to Christians who would dare to read anew the Hebrew texts that should guide our life together—and that inform us, in no uncertain terms, that sometimes our faith should drive us to resist political powers gone awry.[6]

Just as helpful for understanding this point are writings in the New Testament, especially those in the resistance literature of the Book of Revelation, where the state and its governing authorities are characterized not as ministers of God but as "the beast" that makes war on the saints (13:5–7), "the great whore" who demands idolatrous practices (17:1), and "Babylon the great," always eager to reenslave the people of God (17:5).

How were the early Christians to respond to this death-dealing beast—by loving and honoring it? Nowhere does the writer of the Apocalypse counsel the early Christians to love their country, to honor the beast that would slaughter and devour them, or to rush back into the arms of an oppressive Babylon. Instead, the writer calls for patient endurance and commends the type of resistance enacted by martyrs who opposed the idolatrous demands of the Roman Empire.

Make no mistake about it: Christianity *is* resistance, its character indelibly marked by opposition to political powers that undermine the biblical values of peace and liberation.

Christianity is also resistance to economic powers that show contempt for the justice of God. Again, let's return to our ancestors, not to the hyper-capitalist Christians in the United States who hold that the relationship between Christianity and capitalism is as close as that between Marxism and communism, but to the Hebrew prophets we have come to know in Amos, Isaiah, and Micah.

Unlike the pandering preachers of today's "gospel of prosperity," the prophets focused their sights on the evils of economic justice and, more particularly, on the unjust breakdown of an inheritance system that assured wide distribution of land ownership to families who would otherwise fall off the economic map.

Here's the background: As monarchies came to power in Israel, the new kings seized land in order to increase their own royal wealth and to reward their lapping loyalists. Predictably, this oppressive redistribution of land created a new class of wealthy royal supporters and destroyed traditional family-based farms to the extent that many Israelites found themselves in a vicious cycle of poverty, wholly unable to provide for themselves and their hungry children.[7]

When facing this unjust system, the prophets did not counsel the Israelites to be content with the little material goods they had, or to trust that one day God would put two chickens in every pot, or to pull themselves up by their bootstraps and get on with making a real living. Rather, the prophets directed rage-filled words against the unjust accumulation of land and wealth—and against the royals and royalists whose economy blatantly opposed the God who cared for the widow, the orphan, and the poor. Recall the stirring words of Amos:

> For three transgressions of Israel,
>> and for four, I will not revoke the
>>> punishment;
> because they sell the righteous for silver,
>> and the needy for a pair of sandals—
> they who trample the head of the poor into
>> the dust of the earth,
>> and push the afflicted out of the way.
>>> (2:6–7)

> Hear this, you that trample on the needy,
>> and bring to ruin the poor of the land,
> saying, "When will the new moon be over
>> so that we may sell grain;
> and the sabbath,
>> so that we may offer wheat for sale?
> We will make the ephah small and the
>> shekel great,
>> and practice deceit with false balances,
> buying the poor for silver
>> and the needy for a pair of sandals,
> and selling the sweepings of the wheat."
>>> (8:4–6)

Let's return, too, to the early Christians who resisted poverty in their midst, not by earning as much as they could and saving as much as they could and giving away as much as they could within the economic system of their wider society, but by creating a countercultural community that practiced its own economy of grace. Luke depicted this community in a way that must remain deeply offensive to all Christians who venerate private property, the profit motive, and the free market:

> Now the whole group of those who believed were of one heart and soul, and no one claimed private ownership of any possessions, but everything they owned was held in common. . . . There was no needy person among them, for as many as owned lands or houses sold them and brought the proceeds of what was sold. They laid it at the apostles' feet, and it was distributed to each as any had need. There was a Levite, a native of Cyprus, Joseph (to whom the apostles gave the name Barnabas, which means "son of encouragement"). He sold a field that belonged to him, then brought the money, and laid it at the apostles' feet. (Acts 4:32–37)

Again, make no mistake here: Christianity *is* resistance—it's resistance to economic forces that create cycles of poverty which leave people without access to the material goods they need to survive and flourish.

Christianity is also resistance to religious powers that would silence our faith. And here we can easily recall the familiar story of Shadrach, Meshach, and Abednego, our three fiery ancestors who, under threat of being burned alive in the royal furnace, withstood the command "to fall down and worship the golden statue that King Nebuchadnezzar has set up" (Dn 3:5).

When called before the king, who had assumed the role of religious leader exactly when he made his idolatrous decree, the three men buttressed their acts of resistance with sharp words of even greater defiance: "If our God whom we serve is able to deliver us from the furnace of blazing fire and out of your hand, O king, let him deliver us. But if not, be it known to you, O king, that we will not worship the golden statue that you have set up" (Dn 3:17–18). As the story goes, Nebuchadnezzar contorted his face in anger and threw the defiant defenders in a furnace cranked up to its highest levels, but, thanks to God, the three courageous resisters survived the flames.

This beloved story of resistance must have fired up the early Christians who confronted religious authorities opposed to teaching in the name of Jesus, and, indeed, more than a faint echo of the three resisters can be detected in the words of Peter and the apostles as they defended themselves before the high priest of Jerusalem.

The high priest was certainly no fan of the new teaching invading his temple—strange and peculiar lessons about Jesus rising from the dead, about the power of Jesus to heal the sick, and about his indispensable role in human salvation. But Peter and the apostles did not really care much about the feelings of the high priest, and after entertaining his self-serving complaints, they countered, "We must obey God rather than any human authority" (Acts 5:29). With these simple words of resistance, they stood opposed to the highest religious authority of their day and continued to teach and preach in the name of Jesus.

Yes, Christianity *is* resistance—it's resistance to religious authorities who divinize their own roles, practices, and institutions while seeking to silence the new life that Jesus offers even to "uneducated and ordinary men" (Acts 4:13).

I have turned to familiar biblical stories here to help us understand that the theme of resistance is far from peripheral to our Christian faith. Resistance may not always be Christian—many historical movements of resistance have been driven by secular ideologies—but Christianity *is* resistance. That much is clear from even the most casual reading of the sacred texts of our faith, and as you'll see in the pages ahead, Christianity is also much more than resistance to oppressive politics, economics, and religion. It's also resistance to cultural forces that divide Jew from Gentile, slave from master, and male from female. It's resistance to social forces that transform the prophets' dream of watered gardens and full bounty into the most terrifying of nightmares. And it's resistance to ideological forces that elevate a twisted form of individualism over the solidarity called forth by our life together.

Resistance, it turns out, is the very heart of Christianity.

JESUS AND RESISTANCE: REMEMBERING THE KING ON A DONKEY

But let me be honest here and admit that I have been selective in my use of biblical texts when making the rather bold claim that resistance is the heart of Christianity. There are more than a few texts that appear to offer counter-evidence to my claim, and perhaps the most significant of these is the one we find in Romans 13: "Let every person be subject to the governing authorities, for there is no authority except from God, and those authorities that exist have been instituted by God. Therefore whoever resists authority resists what God has appointed, and those who resist will incur judgment" (13:1–2).

Ouch. Perhaps I should just concede that Billy Graham and other conservative Christians are exactly right when they tell us that Christianity breeds patriotism. After all, Romans 13:1–7—and similar texts—does indeed encourage an uncritical stance that respects and honors the governing authorities and their policies.

Unsurprisingly, Christians who favor resistance over nonresistance have quickly sought to explain away or expound on the apostle Paul's very clear counsel that Christians should not resist the governing authorities. Martin Luther King Jr., the most famous Christian resister of the twentieth century, dismissed the text entirely by claiming that it emerged from Paul's faulty belief that the Second Coming of Jesus was just around the corner. Because Paul was wrong about Jesus coming anytime soon, King argued, Christians are now free to resist.[8] And Lee Griffith, perhaps the most prolific Christian anarchist of the twenty-first century, has encouraged Christians to treat the Romans 13 passage with more than a healthy dose of skepticism. "If Paul was urging obedience to rulers," Griffith writes, "what accounts for his repeated arrests and his reputation as a troublemaker?"[9]

The critical points raised by King and Griffith, as well as those flagged by pro-resistance biblical scholars, are undeniably important for understanding the historical context, and perhaps the real meaning, of Romans 13. But it would be absolutely foolish, and downright wrong, for any of us to argue that non-resistance is not a significant part of the legacy of Christianity. All we have to do is look around—non-resistant Christians are everywhere.

You may reply here that non-resistance is not the legacy of true Christianity and that if we want to see real Christianity, at least here in the United States, we need only recall the Christian resistance that came to expression in, among other recent places, the civil rights movement and the anti–Vietnam War protests. That may very well be true. But it's just as true that the legacy of Christianity is fiercely contested and that our faith has given rise, on our very own soil, to an uncritical love for the leaders and policies of America the beautiful.

Unlike King and Griffith, millions of U.S. Christians have accepted Romans 13 at face value, and seeking to be faithful to the word of God, they have embraced an uncritical patriotism that loves and honors both our governing leaders and their commitments in matters of war and peace, economics, religion, and so much more. The historical evidence is clear: Christianity has indeed given rise to a patriotism that decorates our churches with the U.S. flag, that fuses the Bible with the Declaration of Independence, and that fills our sanctuaries with patriotic hymns. Graham was right—Christianity does breed patriotism.

And so how are we to resolve this tension? How are we to respond to the opposed legacies, created in part by seemingly divergent biblical texts? Where are we to turn when settling the question of which legacy we should adopt? How are we finally to answer the question of whether Christianity *is* resistance or *breeds* patriotism?

I propose that we settle the question, at least for our present age of horror, by taking our primary cue from the Jesus of the Synoptic Gospels.[10]

Let's remember the Jesus who fashioned his role and ministry in direct opposition to the political powers that trampled the poor, ignored the cries of the ill, and enslaved men and women for the glory of Rome. When Jesus spoke of his own mission—"The Spirit of the Lord is upon me, because he has anointed me to bring good news to the poor. He has sent me to proclaim release to the captives and recovery of sight to the blind, to let the oppressed go free, to proclaim the year of the Lord's favor" (Lk 4:18–19)—it would have been clear to all who had ears to hear that he set his life in direct resistance to the political power of his day: Caesar enslaves, but Jesus liberates.

Let's return to the Jesus who resisted worldly power by creating a countercultural community marked by humble service. "You know," he told his disciples, "that among the Gentiles those whom they recognize as their rulers lord it over them, and their great ones are tyrants over them. But it is not so among you; but whoever wishes to become great among you must be your servant, and whoever wishes to be first among you must be slave of all" (Mk 10:42–44). The Gentile rulers tyrannize, but the followers of Jesus serve.

Let's recall the Jesus who resisted the emperor by instructing the Pharisees and Herodians, after they had asked him whether they should pay taxes, to "give to the emperor the things that are the emperor's, and to God the things that are God's" (Mk 12:17). Yes, Jesus wanted his questioners to acknowledge the rightful role of Caesar, but his counsel "to give to God what is God's" clearly implied that his hearers should also oppose the emperor when he demands, as he no doubt would, what belongs to God.

Let's think back to the Jesus who dared to resist a deadly threat from Herod Antipas, the political ruler of Galilee and Perea. Knowing of the threat, some Pharisees warned Jesus, "Get away from here, for Herod wants to kill you" (Lk 13:31). How did Jesus reply? He certainly did not say "My Herod, right or wrong," and he certainly did not tell the Pharisees that everyone should love and honor and pray for this would-be assassin. (By the way, there is no report in the Synoptic Gospels or in any other part of the New Testament that Jesus ever once prayed for his political leaders.) Rather, he said, "Go and tell that fox for me, 'Listen, I am casting out demons and performing cures today and tomorrow, and on the third day I finish my work'" (13:32). And with these acerbic words as his guide, Jesus stood up to his crafty, cunning opponent and continued on with his healing ministry.

Finally, let's call to mind the Jesus who subverted the brutality and arrogance of political power by riding a donkey into Jerusalem shortly before his death. This was not a king who ruled from high above the people, who stole land and money from his subjects, who wielded the power of the sword, and who beamed with arrogant pride. "Here," writes Walter Pilgrim, "authority and kingship are reinterpreted in terms of lowliness, service and peacemaking. Here is kingship without violence, national ambition, or imperial dominance."[11] If we would just stop coating Palm Sunday with syrupy sentimentality, we might begin to understand that Jesus' humble entry into Jerusalem, where his beloved followers laid branches before the passing donkey and shouted "Hosanna!" (God saves), was nothing less than a dramaturgical act of powerful resistance to the governing authorities.

Although there is more rich evidence to mine in the Synoptic Gospels, let's stop here and observe that even if we were to concede that there is some counter-evidence (for example, the text that has Jesus saying, "do not resist an evildoer"),[12] we must nevertheless agree that most of Jesus' life and ministry, at least as depicted in the Synoptic Gospels, both embodied political resistance and encouraged his followers to create countercultural communities of resistance—communities that opposed the violence, poverty, and idolatry perpetrated by the governing authorities.

Jesus, it turns out, was no Paul—Jesus *was* resistance. And if the Jesus of the Synoptic Gospels remains the primary source of our Christian faith, the question of whether Christianity *is* resistance or *breeds* uncritical patriotism is now easily settled: The Way of Jesus is the way of resistance to the governing authorities. I could continue on here and make the case that the Way of Jesus is also the way of resistance to certain religious authorities and many other oppressive forces, but I will simply point you to the exciting pages ahead for these themes.

CHRISTIAN RESISTANCE FOR ORDINARY PEOPLE: FROM COMPLICITY TO RESISTANCE IN THE UNITED STATES

If Christianity is resistance, resistance is not just for wild-eyed, long-haired, pot-smoking radicals. Nor is it just for heroes beyond our reach. Resistance is for all Christians, everyday Christians, *ordinary* Christians—it's for you and for me.[13]

Resistance is for two ordinary midwives who dare to think that the pharaoh is wrong when he tells them to kill innocent babies—and it's for ordinary Christians who just know that sometimes the governing authorities are beasts that make war on the saints.[14]

Resistance is for an ordinary shepherd from Tekoa who musters enough courage to tell the powers that be that their economy of royalty, with its unjust accumulation of land and wealth, insults the God of the widow and the orphan—and it's for ordinary Christians who just feel in the deepest recesses of their hearts that they should share their goods with those in material need.

Resistance is for three ordinary men with enough courage to withstand religious authorities who demand allegiance to their human idols—and it's for ordinary Christians who just sense that it's faithful to resist anything human that claims to be divine.

Resistance, at last, is for a Jewish carpenter who rides a donkey into Jerusalem—and it's for all other individuals, however ordinary, who desire to join his countercultural community in this new century.

The need for ordinary Christians to join the way of resistance is fiercely urgent—especially now and especially here in the United States.

Resistance has long been a hallmark characteristic of Christianity in the United States. We need only recall the political sermons of the American Revolution, the abolitionist pamphlets of the nineteenth century, the Anabaptist writings about the world wars, or Martin Luther King Jr.'s "Letter from Birmingham City Jail," to realize the historic intensity and endurance of Christian resistance in the United States.

As these examples suggest, resistance has typically, and most strongly, emerged in Christian theory and practice during periods of international crises or grave domestic injustices—times when a significant core of Christians have perceived their cherished virtues and practices to be under assault in the wider society.

Without sounding alarmist, one can successfully argue that the United States is currently facing both types of crises—internationally, the country is deeply involved in a war that many citizens now oppose; and domestically, the gap between rich and poor, citizens and "illegal aliens," and whites and people of color has only widened in recent years—and that these crises, coupled with the environmental disasters we can read about every day, pose untold dangers to the Christian values of peace, justice, community, and ecology.

But let's not point our finger at others too quickly.

The world beyond our Christian communities is not the only party responsible for the horrors of our new century—we Christians are just as guilty. An unjust war is raging with the complicity of Christians who forget that Jesus came preaching peace. A capitalist economy is widening the gap between rich and poor with the complicity of Christians who forget that Jesus identified himself with the hungry and thirsty. A cultural force of old-fashioned Americanism is demonizing immigrants with the complicity of Christians who forget that we are all "resident aliens." And global warming is wreaking havoc on our planet with the complicity of Christians who forget that the earth is the Lord's.

There are small movements of Christian resistance here and there—countercultural communities like Sojourners in Washington DC, Christian advocacy groups that fight for legislation reflective of our values, and laity groups that protest unthinkable abuses perpetrated by our religious leaders—but if Christianity *is* resistance, the small remnant of resisters, while it gives us hope that all is not lost, is but a stark reminder of the dismal failure of U.S. Christianity in the twenty-first century.

Can we do better? The contributors to this volume certainly think so, and with renewed passion and prayers for the Way of Jesus, they will help us leave behind a life of complicity and take up a Christianity that resists any politics, economics, or religion that serves the powerful rather than those on society's margins or even the welfare of earth itself. And this gets us to the basic purpose of this book—to help ordinary U.S. Christians reflect on the importance of developing and practicing an ethic of resistance for the twenty-first century.

The question of what it means to be a Christian resister in the United States at this point in our history is not easy to answer. It's not enough to say that Christianity is resistance. Yes, we are Christians, and we must resist. But what forms should our resistance take right here and right now? Should we restrict ourselves to building countercultural communities? Or should we seek to change political, economic, and civil society from within? Should our resistance be nonviolent? Or should it sometimes advocate the use of force?

What exactly should we resist as we make our way through this new century? Should we restrict ourselves to resisting the evils identified by the Bible? Or are there new targets of Christian resistance? Should we resist just the governing authorities? Or are there additional forces that demand our resistance?

And what do the rich sources of our faith—especially the life of Jesus, the Bible, and the great cloud of witnesses—counsel us about Christian resistance for here and now? Can we find examples of Christian resistance in our history or in the global community that can help us develop a new Christian ethic of resistance for today's horrors?

I invite you to turn the page and join us as we try to answer these tough questions. But most of all, I encourage you to join us in our hope against hope that we can do better, that we must do better, and that massive resistance is the way for all Christians in our new century.

A final note: Although the topic of resistance suggests that the pages ahead will be negative in tone, you'll soon see that the contributors focus not only on what Christians should resist but also on the community that we would do well to build. We must tear down, yes, but we must also build up. Christianity, after all, is not only resistance—it's also the creation of "the beloved community," the flourishing of peace and justice on earth, and the very presence of the ever-reconciling Spirit of Jesus.[15]

NOTES

[1] News Release Transcript, Crusade Information Service, Billy Graham Team Office, November 17, 1965, Houston Texas, collection

345, box 55, no. 5, p. 1, Billy Graham Center and Archives (BGCA). Graham also stated that we should support the government as long as it is faithful to God, but he never understood the Vietnam War, let alone a host of other unjust federal and state actions, as unfaithful to God. He allowed for civil disobedience, but only when the government denies religious freedom.

[2] Billy Graham to Lyndon Johnson, July 11, 1965, Lyndon Baines Johnson Library.

[3] In his July 11, 1965, letter to Johnson, Graham wrote: "The Communists are moving fast toward their goal of world revolution. Perhaps God brought you to the kingdom for such an hour as this—to stop them. In doing so, you could be the man that helped save Christian civilization."

[4] Press Conference Transcript, March 12, 1968, Black Mountain, North Carolina, collection 24, box 1, folder 8, pp. 8–9, BGCA.

[5] Whether Shiphrah and Puah (or several other biblical characters I will cite) were truly historical personalities does not affect my argument in the slightest. What matters most is that scripture depicts them as heroes of our faith—ordinary people whose lives are commended as exemplary.

[6] For other stories, see Lee Griffith, "Called to Christian Anarchy?" in *God and Country? Diverse Perspectives on Christianity and Patriotism*, ed. Michael G. Long and Tracy Wenger Sadd (New York: Palgrave Macmillan, 2007), 186–191; and Ronald H. Stone, "Resistance to Military Neo-Imperialism," in *Resistance and Theological Ethics*, ed. Ronald H. Stone and Robert L. Stivers (London: Rowman and Littlefield Publishers, 2004), 124–126.

[7] See Bruce C. Birch, *Let Justice Roll Down: The Old Testament, Ethics, and Christian Life* (Louisville, KY: Westminster/John Knox Press, 1991), 261–264.

[8] Martin Luther King Jr., "Advice for Living," in *The Papers of Martin Luther King, Jr.*, vol. 4, *Symbol of the Movement: January 1957–December 1958*, ed. Clayborne Carson et al. (Berkeley and Los Angeles: University of California Press, 2000), 280–281. "Today," King wrote, "we live in a new age, with a different theological emphasis; consequently, we have both a moral and religious justification for passively resisting evil conditions within the social order" (281).

[9] Griffith, "Called to Christian Anarchy?" 193.

[10] Whether Jesus really said the words I am about to cite does not affect my overall argument. What matters most is that the Synoptic Gospels use these words to invite the followers of Jesus into a life of resistance.

[11] Walter Pilgrim, *Uneasy Neighbors: Church and State in the New Testament* (Minneapolis: Fortress Press, 1999), 101. This section of my introduction is partly indebted to Pilgrim's argument that Jesus practiced an "ethic of critical distancing" (37–124).

[12] Pro-resistance biblical scholars have dealt with this text, too; see, for example, Walter Wink, *Engaging the Powers* (Minneapolis: Fortress Press, 1992), 185. Wink argues that the command not to resist evildoers is better translated as "do not resist violently."

[13] I emphasize *ordinary* here not only because most of us are exactly that—ordinary—but especially because the resistant disciples are also depicted as "uneducated and ordinary" (Acts 4:13). Another inspirational source behind my use of *ordinary* is a beautiful book just recently released—Kristina E. Thalhammer et al., *Courageous Resistance: The Power of Ordinary People* (New York: Palgrave Macmillan, 2007).

[14] I am not suggesting, of course, that Shiphrah and Puah, or any of the other Hebrew personalities I refer to, were Christian.

[15] By using the phrase "beloved community," I am drawing especially from the work of Martin Luther King Jr., who stated this about the Montgomery boycott in 1955 and 1956: "It is merely a means to awaken a sense of shame within the oppressor but the end is reconciliation. The end is the creation of a beloved community. The end is the creation of a society where men will live together as brothers" (Martin Luther King Jr., "The Birth of a New Age," in *The Papers of Martin Luther King, Jr.,* vol. 3, *Birth of a New Age: December 1955–December 1956* [Berkeley and Los Angeles: University of California Press, 1997], 344).

PART 1
JESUS AND THE WAYS
OF RESISTANCE

From Resistance to Reconciliation

The Means and Goal of Christian Resistance

Curtiss Paul DeYoung

I met members of the Jerusalem Peacemakers while I was in Palestine and Israel in 2007. The Jerusalem Peacemakers is an interfaith network of religious leaders in the Holy Land developing deep relationships across religious lines. I spent a half day visiting the Jewish settlement of Tekoa with two of their leaders, Eliyahu McLean (an Israeli Jew) and Sheikh Abdul Aziz Bukhari (an Arab Sufi Muslim). Tekoa is an Orthodox Jewish outpost deep in the West Bank located at the ancestral home of the biblical prophet Amos. Palestinians are deeply offended by the construction of these settlements and consider them illegal. The Orthodox Jews who build and inhabit outposts like Tekoa believe that God gave them this land and that they are simply reoccupying land promised to them. The tension between Israeli Jews and Palestinian Arabs in the region of Tekoa is intense.

Upon arrival in Tekoa, Eliyahu and I left Sheikh Bukhari at the car and proceeded to bask in the view of a beautiful canyon located at Tekoa. As we peered across this arid desert

3

canyon, we could just imagine Amos standing where we stood, enraptured by visions and prophetic words delivered by the Almighty. We returned from this mystical moment to discover four young men on all sides of the automobile pointing automatic weapons at Sheikh Bukhari. The village vigilantes were not happy to encounter an Arab in their town and were interrogating the sheikh. Eliyahu informed the armed youth that we were in Tekoa to pay a visit to their revered cleric Rabbi Menachem Froman. While still disturbed, they let us leave.

Word of our visit to this small rural outpost must have spread, because we were soon stopped by a burly police officer who queried us regarding our reasons for visiting Tekoa and asked to see identification. He proceeded to say that he did not need to see the identification of Eliyahu (the Jew), and he returned my United States passport without opening it. While the law-enforcement officer paged through the ID presented by the sheikh (the Arab), he declared that Eliyahu and I were not problems, but pointing at Sheikh Bukhari, the officer proclaimed that he was a problem. Switching to Hebrew, he spoke in an agitated tone about why Arabs were a problem for Israel.

When the police officer paused from his rant, Eliyahu stated that we were traveling together as a Jew, a Muslim, and a Christian to demonstrate that people of different religions could live together in peace. Unexpectedly, the officer relaxed a bit. He shared that he had migrated to Israel from Chile. People of many religions lived as neighbors in his country of origin. Simultaneously, Eliyahu and Sheikh Bukhari burst out with the greeting, "Hola! Cómo estás." The officer laughed, the tension broke with a moment of shared humanity, and he released us to continue our travels.

Our visit to Tekoa, the hometown of the Hebrew prophet of social justice, was an act of resistance against the religious intolerance that marks so much of the world. Traveling together as leaders from three different religious traditions demonstrated an alternative way of relating. Our together-ness did prompt some residents of Tekoa to react angrily to our parable of peace, and yet this moment that began with resistance and produced a negative reaction also ended with a brief moment of reconciliation as we shared a laugh with a "prejudiced" police officer. Christian resistance is not an end in itself. It is a process toward a goal. It seeks the beloved community. The biblical call for reconciliation must always frame the purpose and practice of our acts of resistance.

THE PRACTICE OF RESISTANCE
BY FOLLOWERS OF JESUS

As noted by Michael Long in the Introduction, followers of Jesus must practice resistance. His many biblical examples remind us that such activism is at the core of our "spiritual DNA" as Christians. Twentieth-century theologian Dietrich Bonhoeffer practiced resistance against the Nazis in Germany and their obsessive anti-Semitism. He wrote:

> Whoever wishes to take up the problem of a Christian ethic must be confronted at once with a demand which is quite without parallel. He must from the outset dis-card as irrelevant the two questions which alone impel him to concern himself with the problem of ethics, "How can I be good?" and "How can I do good?" and instead of these he must ask the utterly and totally different question, "What is the will of God?"[1]

According to Bonhoeffer, "the will of God" determines the Christian's view of resistance. This is a confusing notion, es-pecially given that Bonhoeffer was struggling against Adolf Hitler, who was claiming divine sanction for the actions of the Nazis. For Bonhoeffer, it was not enough to claim God's blessing. The boundaries of God's will were held firm by the biblical witness to social justice and reconciliation. Therefore, any act of resistance that does not lead to reconciliation and social justice is not God's will.

What is God's will for Christian resistance in the twenty-first century? This primary query prompts some more precise personal questions: Whom or what do I resist? Should I focus on changing individuals, communities, nations, corporations, or religious institutions? Do I struggle inside existing structures, or from the outside? Do I actively seek to transform existing structures or should I join with others to create an alternative community? Are there forms of resistance that are off limits to Christians? How do I determine what ways are consistent with the gospel and what actions actually contradict the life and message of Jesus? Perhaps the most controversial question we must consider is the use of violence in the resistance of evil. Is Christian resistance always nonviolent? Is there ever a role for violence? If so, how does one determine when and to what degree?

The practice of resistance in the life of Jesus is where Christians must begin for understanding how to resist evil. A brief look at his life will provide a glimpse into how Jesus practiced resistance and answer some of the questions facing Christian activists in the twenty-first century.

BUILDING RELATIONSHIPS AS RESISTANCE

Jesus resisted the popular notion of who was "worthy" of relationship by developing friendships with persons at the margins of society in his day—women, tax collectors, Samaritans, militant activists, people with disabilities, poor people, and working people. Jesus resisted popular stereotypes and unjust social hierarchies through publicly befriending individuals assigned to the margins of society by the societal caste system of his day. Therefore, resistance to injustice begins at an individual level as we choose our relationships. Who are our friends? Whom do we interact with? These simple questions have profound implications for social justice.

Let me return to Tekoa for a moment and speak of the village cleric, Rabbi Menachem Froman. We traveled to Tekoa hoping to gain an audience with this renowned rabbi. Froman is an uncommon Orthodox settler rabbi. He was one of the founders of the Zionist Jewish religious settlement movement in Israel, and yet he changed his mind about Palestinians and became a peace activist. His love for God and the scriptures pushed him toward reconciliation. While he still feels called to live where Amos lived, he wants to live at peace with his Palestinian neighbors. Rabbi Froman wants to share the land. He has said that he does not care if he lives under an Israeli or Palestinian government. Indeed, he was a friend with the late Yasser Arafat, and he has many friends among Hamas religious leaders. He has actively pursued close relationships with those who many would call the enemy.

We did find Rabbi Froman at his home that day. With his long flowing white beard, he looks like a modern-day Amos in Tekoa. When we arrived, he affectionately hugged, many times, Sufi Muslim Sheikh Bukhari. There was an obvious love between the rabbi and the sheikh, and it was clear that by engaging relationships with "the enemy," the rabbi and the sheikh were resisting the idea that separation by religion or ethnicity should be a norm for society. The experience helped me remember that when Jesus said that we should "love our enemies," he was calling for an act of resistance (Mt 5:44).

Our relationships demonstrate our commitment to social justice and reconciliation. Another benefit of direct relationships with people at the margins is the intimate knowledge we gain of the circumstances created by oppression and injustice. Seeing injustice through the eyes of people who are victimized and marginalized allows us more clearly to pinpoint the underlying causes and better know what or whom to resist.

Persons not directly affected by injustice need firsthand contact to grasp the reality of the situation that demands resistance. Even if we confront one type of discrimination, we may not fully understand another form. For example, persons experiencing racism may not fully comprehend the affects of sexism. Close contact is needed with persons experiencing what we do not face in order authentically to propose the appropriate method of resistance.

Many leaders of resistance movements have been raised in settings or have acquired levels of privilege that protected them from the most horrible aspects of oppression. While Moses was born into the home of oppressed Hebrews, he was raised in Pharaoh's palace. Martin Luther King Jr. and Dorothy Day worked against poverty, but they were not trapped in poverty. Both knew the benefits of a privileged education, and so they connected, deeply and personally, with those who bore the brunt of oppression in order to lead with greater understanding and authenticity.

People from privileged backgrounds who become resisters and activists need relationships with persons at the margins so that they can fully understand the purpose and plans for their acts of resistance. They also need solidarity with people at the margins for accountability and their own personal transformation. Choosing to be an activist is easy if it requires no personal sacrifice. In order for social change to occur in a manner that improves the quality of life for poor people, the lives of persons with privilege will likely change. Regular interaction with people at the margins can also transform the value system of privileged individuals. In order to sustain an attitude and lifestyle of social justice, relationships must be long term and deeply felt. The allure of privilege and power is very commanding and so intoxicating. Those of us raised in circumstances of advantage need to engage in such relationships for the extent of our lives if we want to remain committed to God's social justice.

TRANSFORMING CULTURE AS RESISTANCE

In addition to creating a wide web of relationships, Jesus also resisted the cultural images that locked people into injustice. For example, at the healing of a woman who had been bent over for eighteen years, Jesus embraced her as a "daughter of Abraham" (Lk 13:10–17). Jewish men were often referred to as sons of Abraham, but it was extraordinary to call a woman a daughter of Abraham. The grip of patriarchy was relaxed when Jesus introduced the phrase "daughter of Abraham." For another example, recall Jesus' treatment of the Samaritans, who were long relegated to the lower rung of the social hierarchy. Every time Jesus included positive images of Samaritans in his sermons and stories (Lk 10:29–37), he loosened the shackles of bigotry, resisting and reversing the notion of Samaritan inferiority. It must have worked, because today the title Samaritan is used to praise someone's good works. These two examples illustrate how Jesus resisted the bigotry and injustice of a social hierarchy built on gender, race, and socioeconomic class distinctions and cemented into place through cultural meanings.

In 2003 I visited South Africa to speak in four cities on what was called the Jesus Was Black tour. The primary purpose of the tour was to resist and dispel the idea that Christianity is an exclusive faith and to restore the biblical truth that people of all races and cultures are created fully in the image of God. I described how white images became the dominant and exclusive representation of Jesus Christ in every part of the world. I noted that the proliferation of white images of Jesus and biblical characters sabotaged the ability of the biblical message to be heard and embraced in many settings around the world. I shared that some scholars now speak of Jesus as an Afro-Asiatic Jew.[2] And I suggested that a white, exclusive version of Christianity as found in South Africa (and the United States) has been built on heretical notions and political agendas. This is in contrast to the Jesus in the Bible, who said he came to build "a house of prayer for all of the nations" (Mk 11:17).

In most settings the response was mixed and intense dialogue occurred. I asked people to close their eyes and imagine Jesus walking toward them. Then I asked them to describe what Jesus looked like. Most people saw a white man with northern European features. This particularly troubled persons of color. Some struggled with the notion that if humans were created in the image of God, and they as persons of color imagined Jesus as white, what did that say about their own sense of identity and worth? How could they overcome feelings of inferiority enforced and encouraged under apartheid with white images of Jesus Christ controlling their vision of the Divine and who was made in the image of God?

I was told that after some sessions whites reported struggling with the notion of a Jesus who was black. Some said that while they could let go of a white image of Jesus, they could not embrace the idea of a black Jesus. The suggestion was that Jesus was neither white nor black. Interestingly, I never asked anyone to accept an exclusively black Jesus. I just pleaded that they reject the notion of an exclusively white Jesus. I said that Jesus was an Afro-Asiatic Jew—which in the United States does mean, historically, that Jesus would be socially and culturally classified as black (at least one drop of black African blood running through his veins).

Such a reaction in South Africa demonstrates how deep in the psyche and how emotionally charged are our beliefs about blackness as a negative identity. I suggested that if we discovered a picture of Jesus of Nazareth that proved he was black, our faith should not be affected. If we cannot easily love, serve, and embrace a black Jesus, this reveals that our faith is built on the race of Jesus and not on his death and resurrection. One participant at a workshop told me that he had heard a white person say, "If Jesus is not white, then I am not a Christian."

Resisting and dismantling white supremacy is hard and difficult work—especially in the context of our religious faith, where our deepest values reside. In subsequent visits to South Africa, persons who heard these messages have recounted how they rediscovered a lost part of their humanity. Persons of color testified to the transformation that had occurred in their own lives. Their "blackness" was redeemed. They could now fully embrace the fact that they *were* created in the image of God. The "whiteness" of the image of Jesus was used historically to support the notion that whites were superior and persons of color were inferior. Dismantling this lie allowed whites and persons of color to reject a racialized definition of who is created in the image of God.

Jesus resisted stereotypes and transformed cultural images in his day by injecting into the popular culture positive depictions of Samaritans and women ("daughter of Abraham"), and so it is shocking that stereotypes about and cultural images of Jesus himself are what we need to resist in this modern era.

But the good news is that when we resist images in popular culture that are designed to fortify injustice—such as a white Jesus—we release the possibility of liberation and social justice in society. Popular culture and community storytelling often pass on to the next generation tired stereotypes and distorted images that perpetuate injustice—and not just about Jesus and persons of color. We must resist this largely unnoticed process, and we must resist by challenging existing notions and replacing them with truthful information.

Another powerful way to resist ingrained cultural affirmations of injustice is through creating alternative communities. These communities illustrate a different vision for life together. Resistance to materialism can be expressed by a simple and shared communal lifestyle. A commitment to address the roots of poverty can be exemplified by residing in impoverished areas and serving in community development. An egalitarian ethic can be modeled in such a compelling way as to suggest that the time could come when the words *oppressor* and *oppressed* become obsolete terms in the lexicon of society. Alternative communities insert a just option into the public imagination. These communities paint a picture of what is possible. They put flesh on notions of the beloved community and the reign of God.

PUBLIC PROTEST AS RESISTANCE

Jesus practiced resistance to injustice by creating relationships and transforming culture. Jesus also resisted injustice through public protest. The most widely known example is the clearing of the money changers from the Temple. This demand for equal access to the central institution of religion and community governance was so significant and memorable that it is included by all of the Gospel writers (Mt 21:12–17; Mk 11:15–19; Lk 19:45–48; Jn 2:13–17).

Another example of public protest by Jesus is put forth by Marcus J. Borg and John Dominic Crossan in their book *The Last Week*. They argue that the procession Christians celebrate on Palm Sunday was most likely a protest march.[3] The "peasant procession" led by Jesus entered Jerusalem from the east while an "imperial procession" led by Pontius Pilate and his Roman soldiers entered from the west.[4] Borg and Crossan write: "Jesus's procession deliberately countered what was happening on the other side of the city. Pilate's procession embodied the power, glory, and violence of the empire that ruled the world. Jesus's procession embodied an alternative vision, the kingdom of God."[5] Introducing Palm Sunday as a protest against empire ethics would be a great opportunity for congregations to encourage resistance to power politics and unjust societal structures.

There is a long tradition of protest against injustice in the United States. Public protest is the lens through which we often view resistance. Protest by Christians in the United States has led to the right to vote for women and persons of color, the end of legalized segregation of the races and, in a host of other ways, has addressed human rights and challenged various forms of discrimination. Christians have written letters to government officials, boycotted, participated in sit-ins, marched, filled the jails, lobbied, fasted, prayed, and protested in many other ways. The protests have often been unpopular. Some church leaders have decried these efforts when laws were broken, albeit unjust laws. While the practice of protest is more generally acceptable, what issues to protest against or rally for are still hotly debated.

IS VIOLENT RESISTANCE
EVER AN OPTION FOR CHRISTIANS?

If the actions of Jesus are a model for Christian resistance, there are some forms of resistance that do not have obvious support. The question regarding the use of violence in resistance is a clear example. Jesus never used violence. He even died a violent death without resisting violently. Jesus did say, "Do not think that I have come to bring peace to the earth; I have not come to bring peace, but a sword" (Mt 10:34). But this seems more of a rhetorical device to warn his followers that speaking the truth about injustice will divide people rather than create a false sense of peace. When one of Jesus' followers used his sword at the arrest of Jesus in the Garden of Gethsemane, Jesus said, "Put your sword back into its place; for all who take the sword will perish by the sword" (Mt 26:52). In the Sermon on the Mount Jesus proclaimed, "But if anyone strikes you on the right cheek, turn the other also" (Mt 5:39). This text has been the bedrock passage for many who have claimed that nonviolence was the way of Jesus, such as Martin Luther King Jr., Dorothy Day, and many others, including some outside the Christian tradition, like Mohandas Gandhi and Aung San Suu Kyi.

It was the Sermon on the Mount that inspired the pacifism of Dietrich Bonhoeffer, until he chose to join a conspiracy to assassinate Adolf Hitler. Some say he betrayed his Christian faith. Others believe that Bonhoeffer made the only choice he could in order to remain faithful to God. Bonhoeffer had family members working in German intelligence, so he knew about the genocide of Jewish people. As Bonhoeffer saw it, he faced the choice of being a de facto accomplice with Hitler in the genocide or joining a conspiracy to kill one person and hopefully save the lives of thousands. Bonhoeffer wrote, "I am guilty of cowardly silence at a time when I ought to have spoken. I am guilty of hypocrisy and untruthfulness in the face of force. I have been lacking in compassion and I have denied the poorest of my brethren."[6] So Bonhoeffer became a conspirator in a plot to kill Adolph Hitler. He accepted the consequence that his choice "may prevent me from taking up my ministry again later on."[7]

From my reading of Bonhoeffer, I believe that he made a one-time exception to his core belief in pacifism. He had tried all other forms of resistance available to him, and nothing had stopped the atrocity of the Holocaust. After much prayer and soul searching, Bonhoeffer humbly moved forward on his decision, fully willing to accept the consequences and guilt of his actions. Unfortunately, others have used Bonhoeffer's conflicted choice to support violence. President George W. Bush noted Bonhoeffer in a speech supporting his war against terrorism. When people questioned his call for the assassination of President Hugo Chavez of Venezuela, evangelist Pat Robertson cited Bonhoeffer. I was interviewed on an evangelical Christian radio station, and the talk show host implied that Bonhoeffer was an example for Christians supporting the U.S. war in Iraq. In none of these cases did the persons express that they came to their decision only after much prayer and troubled contemplation. None of them offered to accept the loss of employment. None of these persons claiming the words of Bonhoeffer suggested that this decision might bring guilt and that they were ready to accept the consequences in their lives.

On my first trip to the West Bank in the Occupied Palestinian Territories, I encountered an emotion that prompted me to reconsider a strict commitment to nonviolence. After experiencing the psychological impact of check points, military drones, and the wall, as well as observing firsthand demolished homes and destroyed lives, I could viscerally feel the desire to resist this injustice with violence. That was after one day. How would I feel after months or years? Yet I know, as I surmise Dietrich Bonhoeffer knew, that violence breeds violence. Even a violent act that produces just results does not return without a residue of violence in the outcome. Violence is evil.

Nonviolence is the Way of Jesus and the more holy route to justice.

If a Christian ever chooses violent resistance, it must be done in the manner that Bonhoeffer made his choice—as an exception to the rule in a case of extreme human rights abuses, after all other methods have been exhausted and much prayer has been offered, and with a full willingness to accept the guilt and consequences.

RECONCILIATION AS AN OUTCOME OF RESISTANCE

Christian resistance is not an end itself. The purpose of faith-inspired resistance to evil and injustice is to witness to God's desire for peace, reconciliation, and social justice. By doing God's will, we move closer toward seeing the reign of God on earth—the beloved community. At the very least, acts of resistance hold communities and nations accountable to the standard of God's reign. South African theologian and anti-apartheid activist Allan Boesak writes that this "requires us to soberly assess the situation, not from the comfortable seats of power, but from the depths of the pits from where the poor are yearning to be heard. Reconciliation begins truly when the voice from the pit is heard, and when that voice sets the tone."[8] He adds, "If the 'least of these' who are the family of Christ, of whom the church must be the uncompromising defender, are 'content,' in other words, if they have seen and found justice so that *their* human potential stands a chance of fulfillment, then we have succeeded, then we have been obedient."[9]

For resistance to lead to a reconciled and socially just society, the process of resistance must be permeated with the same integrity desired of the final result. The means and the ends are interrelated. Let us briefly return to the discussion of violent resistance. Dorothy Day, Martin Luther King Jr., Aung San Suu Kyi, Mohandas Gandhi, and others would argue that violence cannot be used as a means if reconciliation and a society without violence is the desired end.

Resistance is the process of drawing attention to evil and injustice while pressuring the powers that be to pursue positive social change. Reconciliation is the process of repairing the brokenness caused by injustice. When we can move from resistance to reconciliation, we know that we are closer to experiencing a foretaste of the reign of God on earth. Aung San Suu Kyi asserts, "The quintessential revolution is that of the spirit, born of an intellectual conviction of the need for change in those mental attitudes and values which shape the course of a nation's development. . . . Without a revolution of the spirit, the forces which produced the iniquities of the old order would continue to be operative, posing a constant threat to the process of reform and regeneration."[10] Christian resistance followed by reconciliation seeks to transform the very foundation a society is built upon.

RESISTANCE AS A SPIRITUAL PRACTICE

Resistance was a practice of Jesus. Therefore, as followers of Jesus, we must also be activists for social justice. Like Jesus, our resistance will be seen in our relationships, our attempts to transform culture, and our public protest. When resistance is successful, it will produce reconciliation. Ultimately, Christian resistance is a spiritual practice. If racism, sexism, classism, and other forms of injustice are spiritual issues for Christians, resistance against injustice is a spiritual practice. Resistance is active prayer to God for justice, peace, reconciliation, the beloved community, and the reign of the Almighty on this earth. Resistance is prayer for the will of God. The spiritual practice of resistance, done in the spirit of Jesus, brings renewal. Christian activists must embrace the spiritual disciplines of Bible study, meditation, prayer, fasting, and the like. Activism does not replace the other spiritual disciplines. Yet when resisting evil and injustice in the spirit of Jesus, activists discover that God steps beside them in the struggle with "a gift of inward renewal—a divine calm in the midst of the winds of persecution and prejudice."[11]

NOTES

[1] Dietrich Bonhoeffer, *Ethics* (New York: Macmillan, 1965), 188.

[2] For a discussion of an Afro-Asiatic Jesus and the impact of race and culture on images of Jesus, see Curtiss Paul DeYoung, *Coming Together: The Bible's Message in an Age of Diversity* (Valley Forge, PA: Judson, 1995), 31–62.

[3] Marcus J. Borg and John Dominic Crossan, *The Last Week: A Day-by-Day Account of Jesus's Final Days in Jerusalem* (San Francisco: HarperOne, 2006), 2–5.

[4] Ibid., 2.

[5] Ibid., 4.

[6] Bonhoeffer, *Ethics*, 112.

[7] Dietrich Bonhoeffer, *Letters and Papers from Prison*, ed. Eberhard Bethge (New York: Macmillan, 1971), 162.

[8] Allan A. Boesak, *The Tenderness of Conscience: African Renaissance and the Spirituality of Politics* (Stellenbosch, SAF: SUN Press, 2005), 201.

[9] Ibid., 207

[10] Aung San Suu Kyi, *Freedom from Fear and Other Writings*, rev. ed. (London: Penguin, 1995), 183.

[11] Curtiss Paul DeYoung, *Living Faith: How Faith Inspires Social Justice* (Minneapolis: Fortress Press, 2007), 147.

Finding Jesus in Today's Horror

The Powerful Resistance of Le Chambon

Paula M. Cooey

While dissent is hardly new to political and religious practice and thought, the language of desire may strike modern activists' ears as an alien language. Yet it pervades, at least implicitly, if not always explicitly, in Hebrew and Christian scriptures as prophet and psalmist, along with apostle, yearn, hunger, thirst, and ache for righteousness, justice, peace on earth, and restoration for the whole of creation. Desire for

I thank Fairfield University for inviting me to give the Christopher F. Mooney, S.J., Lecture in Theology, Religion, and Society, which I delivered on October 30, 2007. I presented most of this material under the title "Christian Ethics: Desiring Deeply Enough and Dissenting Widely Enough in the Face of Today's Horror." I also thank my colleague Rabbi Dr. Bary Cytron for putting me onto the story of Le Chambon sur-le Ligne. Last but not least I thank Millsaps College, where I once again presented much of this material in a slightly different form as the Summers Lecture on February 7, 2008. Parts of this material also appear in altered form in my book *Willing the Good: Jesus, Dissent, and Desire* (Minneapolis: Augsburg Fortress, 2006).

God, as well as a yearning to desire what God desires as God desires it, appears in the writings of theologians like Augustine as well as in the meditations and prayers of mystics throughout Jewish, Christian, and Muslim history. I use it now to rehabilitate it and widen it from its more modern restrictions to the erotic, and most important, to emphasize the priority of the dispossessed, effaced "other" in the ethics of Christian resistance. My point is that while the moral agent is significant to ethical discussion in a Christian context, this significance is first, last, and always subordinated to the compelling face of the "others" in whose names and for whose sakes Christians act. Dissent is never simply for its own sake or to demonstrate the moral purity of the dissenter. Let me explain.[1]

THE STORY OF LE CHAMBON

Imagine the world in 1940. The nightmare of World War I notwithstanding, the world is once again at war with itself. There is virtually no location untouched by violence, whether or not it is directly involved in combat. Even though the United States remains on the sidelines at this time, the U.S. economy is war centered, and many U.S. leaders, in spite of isolationist opposition and in some cases support for the Axis powers, consider it only a matter of time before the country will become a direct military ally of Great Britain.

At this time the Axis powers have the upper hand. Most of Europe has fallen or is falling under their control. North Africa has fallen. On the Pacific front the Japanese are taking political and military control of Asia. It is unknown whether Germany, Japan, and their other allies can be stopped. Among rank-and-file North Americans, outside the Jewish communities, there are very few who know of the death camps and the ongoing executions of what would ultimately be estimated as ten million Jews, communists, gypsies, Jehovah's Witnesses, physically and mentally challenged people, and homosexuals. Nevertheless, the news media do make clear that it is a time of carnage and destruction beyond comprehension, an age of horror.

France fell to Nazi Germany in 1940. Whereas the Nazis directly controlled northern France, the Vichy government, in collaboration with the Nazis, took charge of southern France. Le Chambon sur-le Ligne, a small rural village located in the southern mountains near the Swiss border, resisted the Nazis and their collaborators in ways unlike any other French village. The villagers hid Jewish refugees, among others, successfully smuggling them with the aid of forged documents across the border to Switzerland. Scholars estimate that the villagers saved five thousand men, women, and children from the death camps. Not one Jew or other refugee who sought aid there was denied it. Not one villager betrayed either the refugees or the other villagers who sought to save them. Most of the villagers were French Calvinists. But some were Catholic, and others were radical fundamentalists. Their collective success in saving lives also depended on outside assistance from American Quakers, the Swiss Red Cross, and Nazis who collaborated with the villagers. Furthermore, they were not always successful. At one point the SS discovered Jewish children in a boarding school and deported them to concentration camps; all were exterminated. Nevertheless, on another occasion, having been warned in advance of a Nazi raid to occur on a particular Sunday, the villagers hid many Jews in the forests and then packed their Sunday services with Jews and Gentiles alike, right under the SS noses. One pastor, André Trocmé, when interrogated by the Nazis, told them that he knew of no Jews, only of human beings, but that even if he knew of Jews, he would not betray them. Trocmé and his associate pastor, Edouard Theis, later fled Le Chambon to avoid their own extermination. The villagers continued their work without ceasing in the absence of two of their central leaders.

Given the more characteristic indifference, the collaboration, and the direct support and participation of the majority of ordinary European Christians in accomplishing the Axis agenda, how could this resistance on the part of a whole village have happened?

Admittedly, this resistance had its leaders, among them the pacifist, Calvinist pastors André Trocmé and Edouard Theis. In 1940 Trocmé preached:

> Tremendous pressure will be put on us to submit passively to a totalitarian ideology. . . . The duty of Christians is to use the weapons of the spirit to oppose the violence that they will try to put on our consciences. We appeal to all . . . in Christ to refuse to cooperate. . . . We shall resist whenever our adversaries demand of us obedience contrary to the orders of the gospel. We shall do so without fear, but also without pride and without hate.[2]

The parishioners who heard this sermon, along with those villagers who didn't, collaborated with one another across boundaries of internal religious difference, Christian traditions that had historically warred with one another. I have in mind here Catholics and Huguenots, as well as the historical attacks by both on the radical fundamentalists. Indeed, the memories of religious strife and persecution in sixteenth- and seventeenth-century France were still alive some three and more centuries after the actual events. Contemporary social scientists even suggest that for the French Calvinists, resistance to the Nazis drew on memories of Catholic persecution as a resource for empathy with the Jews. (I hasten to add that Calvinists historically committed their own persecutions as well.)

What, then, allowed a conspiracy across these divisions to save the lives of people regarded as nonhuman by most Gentile Europeans in their deeply ingrained, historically practiced anti-Semitism, religious prejudice, homophobia, and ethnic bias? What compelled the villagers to risk their own lives for others?

When later asked by interviewers, the villagers denied any heroism on their parts. They responded to the effect that it was the natural thing to do. One woman, drawing on Matthew 25:40, replied that Christians are simply commanded by Christ to feed the hungry and to offer hospitality to foreigners and other strangers; another, a man, offered that Jews were people of God; yet another man said quite simply that Christians are to love God with all their hearts and their neighbors as themselves. Again and again they stressed individual conscience as the authority for their responses. One interviewer was stunned by the serenity, equanimity, and matter-of-factness with which they told their stories. He emphasized that no one knew specifically what the others were doing, beyond his or her own individual or familial behavior. No one had an overall picture of the resistance itself, and yet each responded cooperatively as if the whole village were a single organism. In short, these were ordinary people who thought they were simply doing what ordinary Christians should do.

I suggest that the village as a whole, its individuals trained, so to speak, by generations of self-discipline, quite simply sought to love what God loves as God loves it. Though the military language is ironic for a pacifist, Trocmé and his fellow Chambonnais were well armed with weapons of the spirit such that they desired deeply enough what God desires and could therefore dissent widely enough to risk all in their own age of horror.

THE OTHER-SHAPED FACE OF JESUS

The villagers of Le Chambon, when interviewed, referred over and over to the claim of Jesus upon their lives as authoritative for their actions. What I want to explore is the place of the figure of Jesus in this drama of participating in God's love, for according to Christian teaching, it is the role of Jesus as Christ to reveal what both the divine and the human look like to those who claim a share in Christian identity. What makes Christians particularly Christian, rather than merely monotheistic, is the centrality of the figure of Jesus to Christian practice. Jesus provides the linchpin, so to speak, on which Christian life and practice depend.

To preserve much needed humility, especially for contemporary, relatively affluent, white Christians, I suggest we begin with the recognition that Jesus' own face is "other shaped."[3] According to early strains of the tradition, Jesus saw himself and his mission reflected in a diversity of faces, especially in the faces of devalued, suffering, and despoiled others, not first and foremost in the moral agent called to serve them.

Recognizing a multiplicity of others, in Jesus' face and Jesus' face in others, is hardly a novel suggestion. It finds its roots in Matthew 25:31–40, Jesus' telling of the great Day of Judgment, when the sheep will be separated from the goats, the very passage cited by the woman of Le Chambon. The text is a difficult passage in its potential for a reading that is triumphalist, exclusivist, dualist, and spiritualized. Such a reading further fits with the so-called Great Commission at the end of the Gospel to make disciples of all nations.[4] For example, the initial image of Jesus is one of kingship, glory, and moral discrimination in that "all the nations will be gathered before him. And he will separate people one from another as the shepherd separates the sheep from the goats" (v. 32). Furthermore it contains a cursing as well as blessing. Within this apocalyptic context one could interpret Jesus' identification with the least of these as a concern restricted to those within his community of followers. Nevertheless, to my mind, such readings are undermined by the ultimate focus of the Gospel as a whole on what the author attributes as Jesus' view of his own identity.[5]

I suggest alternatively an interpretation of the passage in the context of earlier passages that support not only love for the neighbor but also love for the enemy. I also caution, as Trocmé cautioned his parishioners in his sermon of protest, that to love one's enemies means to will their good, not to cower before them in obedience to them. There are additional passages occurring in this Gospel that identify the "least" with children as well.[6] This shift in context allows one to read the text against itself. The central theme of the passage lies in Jesus' surprising claim, appearing in none of the other canonical Gospels, that *he* is to be found in "the least of these, my brothers and sisters" (Mt 25:40). He specifies the least as hungry, thirsty, foreign, naked, sick, and imprisoned (my translation). But though his sense of kinship with the least is clear, he does not seem to require that the "least" particularly identify with him in any way in return. As the specific enumeration indicates, Jesus is not identifying with wealth and power. Moreover, and this point deserves special emphasis, he is not identifying with the servants, those he commands to serve the dispossessed, either. Rather, his identity, his kinship, lies with those altogether outside a dualism of master and servant or slave.

Certainly this kinship defines the kingship to which he does lay claim in ways that explode normal assumptions about power and what constitutes powerful rulers *and loyal servants*. The surprise of his interlocutors evidences a seismic disturbance to their own preconceptions of power. Jesus distinguishes those who will inherit the kingdom of God from those who will not, by their ministry *to* Jesus, as he resides in the "least of these." Jesus locates with those who are served; those who serve them—presumably his followers—are called to serve Jesus in them, not to emulate Jesus' moral agency. Modern christological thinking tends on the whole to identify the true followers of Jesus in terms of whether and how well they imitate Jesus. By contrast, this passage distinguishes them in terms of whether they minister *to* Jesus as an outsider to earthly power of any kind, *including moral power*. Because Jesus as king stands in authority over against all "the nations," including the non-Jewish groups, this designation includes all networks of earthly power and governance, conventionally conceived, sustained, and experienced in terms of the accumulation of wealth and status through cronyism, coercion, exploitation and, just as important, in terms of merit and moral agency.

Jesus' asserted kinship *with* the dispossessed rather than as one who ministers *to* them represents an important shift in focus for what constitutes the significance of ethical acts for Christians today. Note the reversal. Jesus is to be found *in* the outcasts. The outcasts are not to be made like us, not to be domesticated and rendered universal, white humans. We are, rather, to cast our lots with them by ministering to them. It is an especially important shift for those who would identify their actions on the basis of presuming to emulate Jesus. In this passage, to emulate Jesus would be ironically to identify oneself as needy, as in need of ministry. Jesus makes clear here that the significance of what we do as moral agents is, at bottom, not about us, not about the identifications of our own loyalties, affiliations, and egos. Rather, moral agency is first and foremost about the other, in fact, a multiplicity of diverse others, with whom we engage. Those who inherit the kingdom seek and find the figure or face of Jesus in the faces of the otherwise effaced. Those who inherit the kingdom respond to the specific situations in which needy others find themselves, not according to the seekers' own abstracted moral calculus. The least of these, the kin of Jesus, need not identify themselves with Jesus or the seekers and their loyalties. These others may indeed be despicable. Inheriting the kingdom depends on finding Jesus in the other, as is, in all her or his specificity, without requiring reciprocity or accommodation. What is truly God locates in human need and vulnerability. What is truly human recognizes God incarnate in human difference and need and responds to this need.

A CHRISTIAN ETHIC OF RESISTANCE

Taken as a starting place for a contemporary Christian ethic, and only a starting place, recognizing and accepting the otherness of Jesus, seeing Jesus in the faces of otherwise effaced others and responding to their need, addresses a number of contemporary concerns. The narrative focuses ethics first and foremost on the *situation* of the other rather than the intentions of the self, preserving what lies at the heart of Jesus' own human ministry, the centrality of the plight of those in need. In addition, the reference to multiple others also embraces human difference and plurality and permits extension to include whoever and whatever qualifies as "least" in today's hierarchical evaluations of worth, including nonhuman life. Most important, the figure of Jesus found in the faces of the least of these, his brothers and sisters, his kin, by virtue of its rejection of moral pretension and sanctimony, mediates vividly the desire to love what God loves *as God loves it*. It means willing an incomprehensible good for strangers, even enemies, no matter how different or loathsome we may personally find them to be.

The other-shaped face of Jesus transfigures desire in relation to a different order, realm, or kingdom, one I would call an economy of generosity and grace, an ordering of life according to abundance and without closure, what other Christians have called an eternal fullness of being. Such an order challenges every finite, therefore human, presumption to know and to establish permanence on the basis of a presumption to knowledge. We, like the citizens of Le Chambon, are to act in response to the need of others without knowing the full picture, instead simply loving or desiring in faith what God desires.

This desire, insofar as its bearer, by grace, struggles to live out of it, necessarily places one and one's communities, as with that of Le Chambon, in dissent against established authority, as with the Nazi regime and its Vichy collaborators, an authority that I propose to be an economy of scarcity, of self-interest, of self-preservation, of being realistic—precisely because an economy of scarcity presumes to know and assert scarcity as absolute.

This desire emphasizes practice over belief, and in so doing calls for a disciplined generosity within which the Christian as moral agent can act spontaneously in response to immediate circumstances, as well as with sustained compassion over the long haul.

This view of Christian ethics, while it weaves together elements of more conventional ethics—principle, virtue, and utility—shifts the focus from the character and virtue of the moral agent to the primacy of the other as outside all usual binaries of power, including the dualisms of right and wrong, good and evil, master and servant, and therefore even the usual calculations of what determines morality. This shift ultimately places one in the situation of ongoing dissent against all attempts to fix morality in the image of the dominant group writ large as universal.

Even to pose such a shift challenges the authority of the moral agent as conventionally understood in both Christian and secular ethical thinking, for it places at least those who would serve Jesus potentially in the role of moral transgressor by authorizing them to minister to, and perhaps even to cast their lots with, the thief, the mad, the illegal immigrant, the convicted murderer on death row, the sick and dying, the militant, possibly even the terrorist, often understood, rightly or wrongly, as martyr. Thus the villagers in our story went about the business of saving lives by calmly breaking laws against harboring Jews, against forging documents, and against smuggling at the risk of their own lives, their families, and their property without agonizing over right and wrong, good and evil, or their own self-interest. They never asked whether those whom they served merited their service. As one villager declared, the Jews who showed up on their doorsteps were like the Jew in the ditch in the parable of the Good Samaritan. His job, said the villager, was to respond like the Good Samaritan rather than the established authorities, all of whom passed by indifferently or, I would add, put the Jew in the ditch to begin with.

For most Christians this shift sounds a call to reject a world and a self defined by economic, political, emotional, and spiritual scarcity—that is, our worlds and our selves as we normally think of them—in favor of an abundance and generosity that we can hardly imagine and yet are called to join in terms of how we live our quite ordinary lives, through the work we seek and do, the children we rear, the environmental footprint we leave, our political and religious activism, and the way we respond daily to one another. We are not likely to find ourselves in the position of hurling our bodies protectively over young men trapped in subway tracks, like Wesley Autrey, but we can respond to immediate need like a young, white, woman medical student, whose name I do not even know, from Washington DC, who, in the midst of the devastation of Katrina, defied federal and state government restrictions by loading up her van with medical supplies and driving all night to reach New Orleans to open a free medical clinic in a Black Muslim mosque in the ninth ward before even one national guardsman had entered the city.

TWO STORIES OF DISSENT

I conclude with two stories of disciplined dissent, born of a partially articulated, largely unintentional desire to love what God loves as God loves it, stories that I think exemplify what it means to shift focus from the moral agent to the other-shaped face of Jesus. Ironically, I have to focus on the moral agent, in these cases the transgressor, to make my point. In the last analysis, however, the stories are about the others they served.

Rick, the son of missionary parents for one of the Reformed Church denominations, grew up in northern Thailand.[7] He is white.[8] When he went to college in the United States, he joined the Army R.O.T.C. Upon graduation he entered the military and was trained as a member of the Special Forces. It appeared to him at the time he would serve in the Army as a career officer. Having attained the rank of major, however, he grew restless. He went off active duty and returned to school at Fuller Theological Seminary. Upon graduation he was commissioned as a missionary by his denomination and returned to Thailand to continue the work of his parents within the tradition of his childhood. College graduate and army officer turned missionary, Rick was the poster boy for clean-cut American masculinity.

Not long after his return to Thailand, however, he began to slip over the Thai border to Burma, also known as Myanmar, to help refugees. With others, he would relocate small but entire villages of tribes people, as they fled the Myanmar rulers who sought to make them slave labor and who tortured and killed them when they resisted. His task was to help them, according to their wishes, find safety within the Burmese jungle. He brought medical supplies, food, and bibles, and he trained tribes people to work with him in like fashion throughout the region. (There was a longstanding past history of established working relationships between some of the tribes and Reformed Protestant missionaries. In the nineteenth century, at the invitation of the British, Christians from the American Baptist, Disciples of Christ, and Presbyterian denominations had entered the region and succeeded in converting whole tribes.)

As the violence perpetrated by the Myanmar military increased in intensity and frequency, Rick found himself faced more and more often with the dilemma of whether to take up arms in defense of the tribes people he sought to aid. He was honest with his mission board about his dilemma. The board members questioned the use of violence, even in defense of

others, and feared, among other things, an international incident. On very defensible grounds, they forbade him to take
up arms. On equally defensible grounds, Rick resigned.

In his thirties and with a family to support, he agonized
over what to do next. As an evangelical Christian, he saw his
dilemma in terms of trying to discover God's next call for
him. The call came when his sister arranged a meeting between him and legally elected Buddhist leader and Nobel Peace
Prize winner Aung Saung Su Kyi. They met. He gave her his
bible from his seminary days. They agreed to begin working
together to build interreligious and political solidarity among
the tribes with the Burmese who resist the Myanmar government. This is no small feat. The tribes people do not get along
across tribes. Furthermore there exists longstanding enmity
between the lowland, dominant Burmese and the tribes, analo-
gous to the historic relations between Americans of European descent and indigenous Americans. All the same, Rick
now devotes his life to building relations, in spite of a bad
history and deep religious differences. Since his meeting with
Aung Saung Su Kyi, Rick has continued his rescue and support work, using it as a further opportunity to develop structures to bring the disparate, opposing groups together in the
face of their common Myanmar oppressors.

More recently, his work has attracted the attention of the
Myanmar military. Rick's friends in the Thai government have
warned him that the Myanmar government has ordered his
death. Rick continues his work anyway because, to his mind,
this is what God, through Jesus, requires of him. His self-
identification and his language are christocentric. When we
first met, he asked immediately if we might pray together in
the name of Christ. When I said yes, he proceeded to thank
God for sending me to hear his story. Jesus figured heavily in
the prayer as he does in the literature and on a website set up
for Rick's organization, the Free Burma Rangers. His politics, conservative in a traditional sense, quite intentionally
are likewise articulated. To us he gave his critique of the U.S.

government, to which he is highly loyal, in a traditional theological language that adamantly rejects an identification of religion with nationalism as idolatry. For example, he spoke of how the United States is threatened by growing political and economic corruption and deterioration as witnessed by the Patriot Act and its infringement on constitutionally guaranteed rights, as well as the greed underlying its economic policies.

A man of warmth, Rick continues to confront danger with disciplined alertness and composure, skills he developed from his early days as a missionary child, through his career in the military, on into the present. At great risk to his own life that entails the threat of significant loss to his wife and three children, he ministers to the forgotten, violated, and despised of the Burmese mountains. His daily existence challenges religious, political, and economic institutions at every point—in Burma, Thailand, and the United States. The current political climate in Myanmar makes his work all the more difficult and risky.

In a very different vein, immigrants cross daily into the United States from a multitude of countries and for a wide range of reasons. While many immigrants flee overt political oppression and torture, others flee the violence of poverty and seek new opportunities promising better lives for their children. If they cross into this country illegally, they by definition live the lives of criminals in fear of being caught and deported. Those who seek to help them likewise technically break the law.

Ellen (names in the story are changed) and I knew each other mainly over lunch and afternoon coffee at the faculty club at the university where I used to work. Ellen is a Unitarian; she is also white. She and I have talked most often about our children. At the time she and I were meeting for coffee on a regular basis, Ellen was a single parent of two sons, one of whom, like my own son, excelled at Latin. Our boys competed with each other locally and then stood together on the same team at state, regional, and national meets. At the local level their respective high school clubs seesawed back and forth as the top two clubs in the city. Her son's club was headed by a young Taiwanese boy, a year older than our son, who excelled without peer not only in Latin, but also in every other academic subject. Sam, his younger brother Tom, and Judy, his little sister, lived with their uncle and aunt and, outside Latin club events, kept pretty much to themselves. Our boys were casual but real friends to them.

One day Ellen and I discovered that Sam, his brother, his sister, and his mother lived as illegal aliens, their green cards having expired years earlier. They actually lived in a rundown motel operated by Sam's absentee father (from Taiwan) in a rough part of town. The motel catered to prostitutes and drug users and served as a money-laundering operation. The kids stayed with the aunt and the uncle during the week so that they might "legally" attend one of the best high schools in town. We learned all of this because the Immigration and Naturalization Service (INS) was on their trail. In a move reminiscent of the Nazi who alerted the village of Le Chambon of the SS raid, and later that the lives of Trocmé and Theis were at risk, an INS worker warned Sam of an impending raid. As we scurried to figure out how to deal with this situation, the INS raided the motel and seized the family, except for Sam, who fortuitously happened to be away from home at the time. The mother was locked up in jail, and the children went to juvenile detention as they all awaited deportation. Sam had escaped but had nowhere to go. If he returned to his aunt and uncle (who were legal), the INS would find him and deport them. Sam called me from a phone booth, and I got him to our house, where he stayed for about three weeks while Ellen and I, with others, figured out what to do next.

Ellen is a genius at solving problems. She connived with the registrar of the school where we taught to get Sam admitted to the university. After three weeks at my house in August, he began life as a first-year student in the dorm, hidden in plain sight, still illegal. At this point we had no idea where the money to pay for this would come from or how to make Sam legal. We ultimately found an immigration lawyer who took on the case for the whole family pro bono. Meanwhile the president of the university got wind of the situation and was initially furious with us. He later came around and persuaded a trustee to finance Sam's education. The registrar traveled with Sam to Canada to get a new green card so that Sam could legally enter the United States and remain here as a student. The lawyer, who habitually takes on such cases, managed to work out a deal, with the consent of Sam's mother, that he and his brother, Tom, would be allowed to remain in the country under the sponsorship and legal guardianship of Ellen. The mother and, at the mother's insistence, her daughter, Judy, would be deported to Taiwan and reunited with Sam's father. In spite of Ellen's efforts, we failed to convince the mother that Judy should stay with her brothers so that she, too, might get a good education and a shot at a better life.

It took Ellen some time to work through taking on such a tremendous responsibility, one that I knew right away our family could not possibly have assumed. (At that time I could see only scarcity.) After some thought, however, she agreed. She essentially redefined her family by committing herself and her two biological sons to two more sons. (This commitment would have included a daughter as well, had things turned out differently.) She has since seen all four boys grow into young adulthood. She got them through college. All four boys had to get jobs, find scholarships, and learn to be resourceful. Sam and his brother, Tom, proceeded on to postgraduate degrees, as did Ellen's older biological son; her younger son went on to a career in the military. She has witnessed all of their marriages as well. Sam and Tom have maintained their relationships with their family of origin but have managed, in no small part thanks to Ellen, to escape entanglement in their father's criminality. Instead of deportation, they got a second chance at an altogether different life with a second family. Ellen treated them just like her other two sons.

I do not know where Ellen found the emotional and financial resources at the time, but find them she did. What was initially and temporarily a clandestine team effort, fraught with legal and moral ambiguity, became for her a full-time responsibility for some years that then turned into a lifetime commitment. She took a stand against several different systems and norms—the immigration system, the legal system, the prevailing academic system, and most important, the norm that family is first and foremost defined by biology. As a single mother, she put her own biologically defined family at no small risk, at first briefly because of the illegality in which we were all involved, then on a much longer-term basis because of the financial and emotional commitment she personally took on. Most important, Sam and Tom found new lives beyond anything they could have imagined before Ellen took them in.

HUMILITY AND RESISTANCE

There is no single recipe for the disciplines that deepen and widen our desire for the good, understood in Christian terms as loving what God loves as God loves it—nor a one-size-fits-all form for the dissent it produces. Rick and Ellen are ordinary people, trained to certain virtues and habits by their religious traditions, and, in Rick's case, ironically, by his military tradition. Both simply responded and continue to respond to the circumstances that befall them with an amazing generosity and a clear focus on the needs of others. Rick's responses to the tribes people are altogether outside the law. Ellen's responses to the illegal immigrants who became her sons also placed her initially and for some time to follow at odds with the law, not to mention the prevailing culture. Rick and Ellen did not intentionally desire for their lives to turn out the way they did; rather, they began with different intentions, hopes, and dreams and ended up winging it, so to speak, in an oddly disciplined way. While it has not been easy for either of them or for their families, it has hardly been drudgery either. Quite the contrary, they each appear to be borne by a peculiar inner joy.

For the rest of us many questions still remain. Will we as Christians continue to stand with our Jewish brothers and sisters against anti-Semitism? Will we as Christians stand together across our own internal divisions and extend special hospitality to our Muslim brothers and sisters in the face of anti-Muslim and anti-Arab extremism in our own government as well as in our own religious institutions? Will we as a people, as citizens of the United States both religious and secular, as members of a wider, global human race, regardless of our religious affiliations or lack thereof, develop sustained compassion, the kind needed to address our deeper and more prolonged disasters of immigration, global warming, rebuilding New Orleans for the people who once lived there *on their terms*, ending the war in Iraq, finding peace in the Middle East? In short, will we resume a forgotten task of building a genuine democracy that seeks freedom and justice from the bottom up, at home as well as abroad? Regardless of our individual answers, ordinary people of secular and religious faiths alike take on these tasks daily even as social institutions, often no longer reliable, resist transformation and crumble around them.

In our own contemporary age of horror, those of us who are middle-class, white Christians in particular have largely thought of Christian ethics in terms of how to become more like Christ as the supreme moral agent, most often projected in our own image. Simply consider the numerous images of a European-looking Jesus plastered all over the walls of our churches. An ethic grounded in the other-shaped face of Jesus as Christ provides Christians with a genuine alternative to these white, middle-class projections of the Christian self, particularly the white Christian self, as the universal human, in the name of a universal God who remarkably resembles white humanity as God incarnate. It further allows white Christians an alternative, creative role in willing the good in a secular society. If we discover what is truly human—among other things human need and vulnerability—and what is truly divine—God's incarnation in that need—in ways that call to us to minister humbly to God rather than to act as if we were gods, if we discover the very image of the Word become flesh in the dispossessed other, we find God in all created particularity. If the other-shaped face of Christ never rests in a single, absolute location, in a single face, a single ego, then the figure of Jesus shines *in difference itself*, not in spite of it.

Right now Christian ethics based on the imitation of Christ plays an inadvertent, treacherous role in the failure to accept difference, to accept otherness, on its own terms. However unintended, this presumption plays its own role in the perpetuation of horror. I think an ethic of seeking and finding Christ first and foremost in the face of the dispossessed other—irrespective of race, class, gender, age, sexual identity, religious or nonreligious identity, social status, or loyalty to our own values—provides a rehabilitation of desiring what God desires. Humility before the other requires spiritual and ethical practice, a hallowing of daily life that fits one to respond spontaneously, to improvise in the midst of ever-changing circumstances, to transgress where necessary. Such practice constitutes the widening and deepening of one's desires and requires the courage of a life of ongoing protest, dissent, in the face of human-defined scarcity. Such humility may surprisingly and ironically even teach us to find the other-shaped face of Christ lastly within.

NOTES

[1] See *Weapons of the Spirit*, documentary, directed by Pierre Sauvage (New York: First Run/Icarus Films, 1988, ©1986); and

Philip P. Hallie, *Lest Innocent Blood Be Shed* (New York: Harper Perennial, 1994).

[2] André Trocmé, as quoted in *Weapons of the Spirit.*

[3] My understanding of the other-shaped face of Jesus is heavily indebted to French Jewish philosopher Emmanuel Levinas, though not without qualification. See in particular, Emmanuel Levinas, *Totality and Infinity*, trans. Alphonso Lingis (Pittsburgh: Duquesne University Press, 1969).

[4] As my colleague New Testament scholar Cal Roetzel (formerly of Macalester College, now at the University of Minnesota) points out, the Greek term translated as "nations" might be better translated "Gentile groups," seeing as the concept of nation is a relatively modern one.

[5] For an example of this interpretation, see J. Andrew Overman, *Church and Community in Crisis: The Gospel according to Matthew* (Valley Forge, PA: Trinity Press International, 1996), 339–352.

[6] See related passages from the Sermon on the Mount (Mt 5—7), becoming a child (Mt 18:1–5), and summarizing Torah, the Law (Mt 22:37–40). See also Krister Stendahl, "Matthew," in *Peake's Commentary on the Bible*, ed. M. Black and H. H. Rowley (New York: Thomas Nelson and Sons, 1962), 769–798.

[7] I met Rick (not his real name) in Thailand in early March 2003, while working on a research project unrelated to this book. I interviewed him in his home at great length, then corroborated as much as I could of his story through other sources. These sources included local colleagues and peers of his, a member of the mission board of his denomination who served at the time that he and the board negotiated an amicable parting of the ways over the issue of arms, websites representing the organization he has helped form and with which he presently works, and newspaper coverage of this organization. I asked for and received his permission to use the interview in my own work.

[8] I racially mark the white people to counter the phenomenon of assuming whiteness as normative, in contrast to other ethnicities and races that go marked under the rubric of people of color. White names distinctive characteristics, attitudes, and histories that are no more and no less universal than, say, black. In my mind, to name whiteness is to own up to certain configurations of power that produce white racism. This would hold for other distinctions along lines of gender, class, and sexual orientation as well.

Christian Resistance in the United States

A Short History

Jeff Bach

The story of resistance to political, economic, and religious domination and violence in the history of the United States is frequently a story of minority people and groups. These stories raise voices of hope that alternatives to "power over others" are possible and beneficial, if not always chosen. Threads of resistance run throughout the history of the United States and back to its colonial era. This chapter provides a brief historical context for past voices of Christian resistance. These alternative voices have witnessed that violence, conquest, and wealth are neither preordained by God nor inevitable for survival. Indeed, the stories of those who sought alternative religious and social visions offer insight to paths to compassion and fairness.

This chapter surveys historically only some selected themes related to the rest of the book. The treatment of these themes and selected religious groups is only suggestive, not comprehensive. Because the focus of the book is on the United States, this chapter explores groups of people within that geographical area, even though some stories unfold in the colonial era. These brief accounts of resistance do not suggest an organic continuity among them all. They simply indicate that in the United States there are multiple threads over time creating alternative models of faith, power, and the use of wealth that differ from many typical stories of America that portray violence as necessary and amassing wealth as the natural outcome for the blessed.[1]

TRANSPLANTED CHRISTIAN FAITH AND LEGAL STATUS

American elementary school pageants in November would be very different if children portrayed not sentimental scenes of Thanksgiving feasts but Roger Williams's banishment and departure from Massachusetts in October 1635 and the harrowing winter that followed. Williams criticized the notions of the Massachusetts Puritans that legal statues should establish a Christian moral order and enforce it. Banished, he founded Providence, Rhode Island, in April 1636.[2] Although he briefly embraced the Baptist faith, which linked the adult baptism of believers to a church constituted only by those responding to God's grace, he came to believe that even the Baptists' view was inadequate for the kind of church he sought. A complex man, Williams also criticized the Quakers for their beliefs, especially their pacifism, and attempted to curtail their influence, even as he granted them asylum in Rhode Island. However, his experiment in Rhode Island signaled a different attitude toward religion within the public realm from that provided by either the Puritans in New England or the Church of England in Virginia in their settlements. As England struggled in the throes of civil and religious war in the midseventeenth century, Roger Williams resisted using legal code to set worship and religious life in order.

Although one might not think of George Calvert (1580–1632), the first Lord Baltimore, or Roman Catholics as a minority, in the English context they were. Calvert converted to Catholicism in 1625, and, on land granted him by King James I for faithful service to the crown, he, with his son Cecil Calvert (1606–75), established Maryland.[3] When the first settlers arrived in 1634, the Calverts hoped to establish a haven for English Catholics and to make a profit. Because Cecil Calvert, the second Lord Baltimore, wanted a more amicable relationship between Catholics and Protestants than conditions allowed in England, Maryland's resident governor Leonard Calvert (brother to Cecil) pursued policies that were friendly to Protestants. Ultimately, though, the Church of England prevailed in Maryland in 1691, when the charter for Maryland was taken from the Calverts. It was reinstated to them when the fourth Lord Baltimore joined the Church of England in 1715.

William Penn created the most remarkable experiment in Christian and even religious pluralism of the colonial era when he established Pennsylvania in 1682. As a member of the Religious Society of Friends (Quakers), he offered a home in his colony to a wide variety of minority dissenting groups from the Continent and from England, tolerating also Catholics and Jews. Not only did Penn offer toleration, but he also actively courted religious minorities, especially among the Germans, Swiss, and Dutch, to settle in his colony. At the same time, he attempted to deal fairly and peaceably with the native populations.

Most of the colonies in North America repeated patterns from Europe of legally establishing religions. However, some Christians found in their faith the motivation to provide asylum to dissenters and at times to those outside their own views.

RESISTANCE TO VIOLENCE

Quakers pioneered not only in toleration, but also in governing with a commitment to pacifism, that is, avoiding war and violence to back up their government in Pennsylvania. The

Quaker experiment endured amazingly well for about seventy-five years, until Quaker representatives in the Pennsylvania assembly withdrew from government on the eve of the French and Indian War (the Seven Years' War) in 1755.[4] Until the Quakers surrendered their majority in the colonial government in 1755, Pennsylvania reportedly experienced no major battles between its native residents and incoming migrants.

Pacifism was not limited to Quakers in the United States.[5] A long thread of Christian-based pacifism runs through the fabric of U.S. history, although it is definitely a minority voice. The Mennonites, Amish, and Brethren, whom the Quakers invited to Pennsylvania, were also pacifists because of their faith in Jesus Christ. The Schwenkfelders, a small religious minority from Silesia who arrived in Pennsylvania in 1734, likewise maintained pacifism formally until the 1940s. The Moravians observed a kind of pacifism.[6] Members of the Community of True Inspiration (the Amana Society) likewise were pacifists when they arrived in the 1840s. The Hutterites, a communal Anabaptist group that migrated to the northern Great Plains in the 1870s, also maintained their pacifism, a characteristic since their organization under Jakob Hutter in Moravia in 1533.[7]

Many of the small religious groups of Germanic background were severely tested in their pacifism in the two world wars of the twentieth century, especially because Germany was the enemy. Many groups modified their earlier stronger pacifism. The Mennonites, Amish, and Hutterites fared best in preserving high adherence rates to their peace witness. The plain, or Old Order, groups among the Brethren and Mennonites, who are theologically the most conservative, enjoy the highest rates of pacifism because they interpret their peacemaking as a biblical mandate of their faith. They also hold high expectations that members of their groups will observe the religious teachings of the groups.[8]

Threads of pacifism emerged in other religious settings in the late nineteenth and twentieth century. As the Pentecostal

movement took shape, some groups initially adopted pacifism because they considered it a teaching of Jesus and the
result of the Holy Spirit's work. Some Pentecostals even participated in Civilian Public Service during the 1940s.[9]

In the Roman Catholic Church, Dorothy Day is credited
as the galvanizing force to raise a Catholic voice of Christian
pacifism.[10] After her conversion in 1927, Day combined the
pacifism of Jesus in the Sermon on the Mount and her critical
reading of Catholic just-war theory to oppose war. This new
religious motivation mixed with her previous experience as a
radical socialist. As founder of the Catholic Worker Movement, Dorothy Day blazed a trail of pacifism that more American Roman Catholics could follow, combining activism with
Christian pacifism, which had always had a home in Catholic
monasticism. In 1962, Eileen Egan and other Catholic pacifists influenced by Day formed the American Pax Association
at the height of the Cuban missile crisis. By 1972 the group
became Pax Christi USA after affiliating with Pax Christi International. Catholic peace workers all around the world in
the latter half of the twentieth century continued to voice resistance to war and violence. Pope John XXIII's 1963 encyc-
lical *Pacem in terris (Peace on Earth)* and Pope John Paul II's
support for peace and economic justice expanded the criticism of war articulated by Pope Benedict XV during World
War I. Thus voices of resistance to violence have come from
the centers of power in the Roman Catholic Church as well
as from the edges.[11]

The historic peace churches—the Quakers, Mennonites,
and Brethren—sponsored Civilian Public Service during World
War II. This program was the first legally authorized alternative to performing military service. Prior to Civilian Public
Service, religious peace groups had to petition for exemp-
tion each time a war came in the United States. The peace
churches did this regularly, from the colonial era through
World War I. Civilian Public Service embodied the positive
work that the member churches and participants saw as the

faithful engagement with good that came from resisting war. Civilian Public Service included many public works projects in forestry, soil conservation, and medical assistance. Some assignments were more risky than others, and among the more dangerous programs was the University of Minnesota Starvation Project directed by Dr. Ansel Keys. Volunteers from Civilian Public Service were subjected to a twenty-four-week period of starvation followed by controlled feeding for recovery over twelve weeks. The goal of the government study was to research the effects of starvation in order to help survivors of the war.[12]

From early beginnings by the Quakers, through the witness of the historic peace churches, Catholics, and other Protestant minorities, alternative models of peacemaking in the face of violence have never been absent from the history of the United States.

RESISTING RACISM

Europeans colonizing in North America typically brought with them attitudes of their superiority over indigenous peoples. These attitudes and behaviors were manifested toward the Africans that were forced into labor here, and they gave rise to patterns of oppression and injustice identified by the term *racism*. Although racist attitudes and economic and political patterns dominated the settlement of North America, occasional variations showed hints of alternatives.

William Penn and the Quakers attempted to form friendly and fair relationships with the native inhabitants of Penn's colony and in other colonies where they settled. Another religious group in Pennsylvania and later North Carolina, the Moravians, likewise tried to create positive relationships with a variety of native groups.[13] Admittedly, the Moravians wanted to convert native peoples to Christianity, which may signal a kind of racism to some modern observers; however, the Moravians wanted to convert white Europeans to their views also. In several areas Moravians attempted to understand indigenous languages and social patterns in ways that few other Europeans attempted. For example, Moravian records of their interactions with the Delaware (Lene Lenape) and Cherokees, including collections of vocabulary, evidence at least some contrast to the patterns of conquest that prevailed in America.

The attitudes and behavior of European settlers toward Africans and African Americans gave rise to deep and long-lasting roots of racism in America. Again, some religious groups showed signs of different patterns. In the seventeenth century, for example, the Quakers did not unanimously oppose slavery. The change took place in the eighteenth century. Elizabeth Buffum Chase, a Friend in Rhode Island, formed the Female Anti-Slavery Society in Fall River, Rhode Island, in 1735. Not until 1780 would the New England Yearly Meeting of Friends prohibit slavery altogether among its members. John Woolman (1720–72), a Quaker from New Jersey, traveled extensively among Friends beginning in 1746, advocating, as Elizabeth Buffum had done, for an end to slave holding.[14]

Two denominations that found shelter in Pennsylvania prohibited slavery from the time of their beginnings. The Mennonites and the Brethren (the largest of the Brethren groups is the Church of the Brethren) forbade the purchase of slaves and disciplined members who did so. In 1688 some Quakers and Mennonites in Germantown (now a part of Philadelphia) raised a complaint against slavery with the Philadelphia Yearly Meeting of Friends. Unfortunately, that protest resulted in no action to prohibit slavery.[15] Later, in the eighteenth century, the Quaker John Woolman told of a Mennonite in York County, Pennsylvania, who slept in an open field rather than stay in the home of a slave holder. The Mennonite man said he could not stay in a home where the would-be host would not offer the same quality of lodging to his slaves.[16] The Brethren printer and minister Christopher Saur II used his newspaper in 1761 to condemn slavery and exhort his readers not to participate in slave holding.[17] The Brethren, who reorganized in Pennsylvania in 1723, and the Mennonites, who had arrived in 1683, both prohibited slavery from their earliest years. At the same time, they were reluctant to participate in abolition societies.

African Americans raised their voices against slavery and racism as well. Sojourner Truth and Frederick Douglass were just two examples of powerful African American speakers and writers who denounced slavery and advocated equality for African Americans.[18] The majority of the actual work to run the Underground Railroad also came from African Americans. Fugitive slaves sometimes sought informal help from other African Americans, whether or not they were part of the Underground Railroad.[19]

On the long journey from the Civil War to the civil rights struggles of the 1950s and 1960s, African American leaders and groups worked to overturn the lasting effects of racism. Segregation and white supremacy, often appealing to Christianity for support, survived intact after the Civil War, perhaps deepened by the policies of Reconstruction.[20] By 1908, African American thinkers and activists, including W. E. B. Du Bois, formed the NAACP to unite their voices and efforts to overcome the reverses inflicted by Jim Crow laws, vigilante violence, and white indifference.[21] These people and many others, often shaped by Christian faith and black churches, witnessed to a different way of valuing people of all racial and ethnic identities prior to the civil rights movement after World War II. While racial tensions persist in the United States, the legacy of alternative views offers stories from which to build different understandings of diversity.

LIFE TOGETHER: RESISTING INDIVIDUALISM

Another thread of resistance in the fabric of Christian experience in the United States has been alternative social structures. In place of the myth of the American pioneer hacking out an independent existence for the nuclear family on the frontier, throughout the history of the United States communities have formed for interdependence and shared religious visions. Economic necessity often played a role in these communities alongside religious idealism. Even with economic necessity, religious groups have often seen alternatives to the myth of individual self-sufficiency. A few of the many communal experiments illustrate some of these efforts.

Some of the communal groups began by design. The earliest sustained communal group in North America was the group of followers of Jean de Labadie who settled at Bohemia Manor in eastern Maryland in 1683. Their community lasted about forty years. A smaller group, led by Johannes Kelpius, settled along the Wissahickon Creek in Germantown in 1694. The Ephrata Community, founded by Georg Conrad Beissel in Lancaster County, Pennsylvania, in 1732, was a larger and longer-lasting enterprise.[22]

The followers of Mother Ann Lee, who eventually were known popularly as the Shakers, did not arrive in 1774 from England to form a spiritual community with a communal economy. Only after the death of Ann Lee did one of her successors, Father Joseph Meachem, begin to gather the believers into "Gospel order," establishing communal congregations.[23] The United Society of Believers, as the Shakers were formally known, formed communities from Massachusetts to Kentucky and temporarily in Florida. The life in community reflected the spiritual goal to resist singular definitions of family and to resist what the Shakers saw as the root of sin—sexual desire. The Shakers have proved to be the longest-lasting religious communal group in the United States.

Some religious communities began more pragmatically for economic survival. The followers of Georg Rapp began to arrive in Pennsylvania in 1804, following their leader and an advance party.[24] They formed a communal settlement, the Harmony Society, about thirty miles north of Pittsburgh in 1805. In 1814 they formed a new settlement in Indiana named

New Harmony, and in 1824 they moved back to Pennsylvania. Their diversified economy of agriculture and trades led to prosperity and reinforced common religious objectives.

In a similar manner the Community of True Inspiration came to the area near Buffalo, New York, in 1844 under the direction of its prophet, Christian Metz. It adopted a communal economy at this time.[25] The community moved to Iowa in 1855 to form the Amana Society. In both cases the religious groups pooled their resources and labor to create communities that sustained their communities of faith.

While many of these groups experienced difficulties that made it difficult to sustain their communities, they also demonstrate that a variety of models of interdependence run through U.S. history.

CONSUMERISM

Voices of resistance to luxury and consumption have often arisen from Christian convictions about wealth. The critique of consumption was all the more important in a nation that was primarily agricultural until the twentieth century. Although luxury goods were often either not available or not affordable, simpler living often had deeper motives than just pragmatic ones.

Some of the early patterns of communal life were as much grounded in economic pragmatism as in religious motivation. Groups like the Ephrata Community, the Moravian settlements like Lititz and Bethlehem (in Pennsylvania), the Shakers, the Amana Society, for example, all survived in their originally rustic contexts with the help of shared labor and housing.

Some religious groups did not adopt formal communal patterns of living but had strong ethics of mutual aid and shunning luxury goods. The Amish have become perhaps the most recognizable of these groups in the twenty-first century. Behind the cliches of barn raisings, a strong ethic of mutual economic assistance prevails. At the same time, the Amish struggle with the market economy. Their sense of entrepreneurship and interaction with both retail economy and tourism industry all point to the interaction between participation and critical distance for the Amish.[26]

In some ways the temperance movements in America can be seen as resistance to a specific type of consumerism. The movements carried a passion for the improvement of living conditions, especially for women and children. While often stereotyped as movements of sheer social control, temperance movements raised concerns about the loss of limited resources to consumption of alcohol.[27]

Dorothy Day and the Catholic Worker Movement raised not only a Christian voice of peace in resistance to war but also a Christian voice against the effects of industrialism on the laborers who powered it. In some ways the Catholic Worker Movement objected to industry "consuming" the lives of its workers. Grounded in a life of prayer and the sacraments of the Roman Catholic Church, Dorothy Day and the Catholic Worker Movement provided a hopeful critique of injustice in an industrial economy.

In a post-industrial society facing the ecological consequences of both industrialism and consumerism, Christian voices of resistance to consumption give alternatives for reshaping faithful responses in the present and future.

FOR THE BEAUTY OF THE EARTH: HINTS OF ECO-JUSTICE

A thread of concern for treatment of the environment sometimes runs alongside some of the groups that explored communal ways of living or resisted individualism. However, these traces of concern for the environment do not represent a fully developed concern for ecology. Among farmers of German and Swiss background, and in groups like the Amana Society

(Community of True Inspiration) or Shakers, there was concern not to deplete the land where they lived. However, they obtained or cleared land for farming, regardless of what its previous ecosystem had been. The awareness and concern over altering ecosystems and the question of the reversibility of those changes were not well-developed prior to the twentieth century.

Still, some unusual examples show up. The Ephrata Community in Pennsylvania experimented with a ban on the use of animal labor for farming and with a vegetarian diet. Its founder, Conrad Beissel, was preoccupied with the violence of animal sacrifice in the Old Testament scriptures. His belief that conversion and spiritual rebirth reoriented one's life led to speculation that it might also alter how Christians treat animals.[28] These experiments seem not to have lasted long and were probably not shared by the non-celibate members of the community. Nonetheless, they represent a questioning of assumed normative patterns of farming with animal labor.

The vocabulary of eco-justice in those terms is relatively recent in the debate of social ethics. Some Christian groups have used the concept of stewardship to refer to an ethic of caring well for land and its resources. However, much of the language of stewardship for Christians has been related to farming, which has significantly altered geographies, watersheds, and waterways, as well as plant and animal populations.

BORDERS

Resistance to borders has been a complex question in the history of the United States both before and after its founding as a nation. Various indigenous peoples did not have fixed concepts of boundaries, even if they had geographical areas that were their common place of residence. European nations, including Spain, England, Russia, and France, have settled or claimed parts of the land through the centuries. The Netherlands and Sweden held colonies here briefly. Many Europeans treated the original inhabitants of the land worse than they treated foreigners back in Europe. In addition, Europeans forcibly brought Africans to this land through the slave trade but denied them and their offspring citizenship. So within the geographical space of the American colonies, and eventually the United States, several segments of the population were initially denied the status of citizen within the boundaries where they resided.

Meanwhile, the nineteenth and twentieth centuries saw continued waves of immigration primarily from Europe but also from Asia, Africa, and South America. Families already established in the United States sometimes helped newly arriving relatives. The Roman Catholic Church, for instance, developed extensive networks to help new arrivals from Catholic lands.

The United States has often struggled between fear of foreigners and a willingness to offer a new homeland. Fear of foreign languages has fueled political attempts to reinforce English as the only permissible public language, from attempts to curtail the use of German in colonial Pennsylvania to efforts to suppress native languages during the nineteenth and twentieth centuries, or to suppress Spanish in the late twentieth and early twenty-first centuries. The United States has alternated between limitations on immigration and welcoming refugees.

In the twentieth century various religious groups responded to others seen as foreigners. American Friends Service Committee and Mennonite Central Committee were both formed early in the twentieth century, the latter to help primarily Mennonites from Russia displaced by the revolution.[29] During World War II, Quakers and Brethren, later joined by American Baptists and Lutherans, helped to resettle thousands of Japanese American citizens who were forcibly interned in 1942 by the U.S. government. Over 110,000 Americans of

Japanese descent in Washington, Oregon, and parts of California and Arizona were ordered into internment camps, ostensibly because they represented a risk to national security. The detainees were resettled in Chicago, Brooklyn, Cincinnati, Cleveland, and Minneapolis by the churches mentioned above. The backlash against the effort was especially strong when New York's Mayor La Guardia tried to halt the effort. This small band of Christians resisted the injustice done to fellow citizens within U.S. borders.[30]

After World War II many Protestant denominations affiliated in the service agency known as Church World Service, helping to resettle people displaced by the war to the United States. Catholic service agencies have engaged in similar ministries, as well as reached out to the growing population of Hispanic workers coming to the United States. In recent decades both Church World Service and Catholic service organizations have helped refugees from southeastern Asia and Africa to come to the United States. Congregations and parishes scattered across the nation have participated in these efforts, sometimes making room in their communities for one family, sometimes for several. While some voices speak their fear of foreigners in the United States, some Christians resist that pressure and seek ways to offer shelter and a new home.[31]

CONCLUSION

All of these stories are merely suggestive of the complex patterns of resistance to power, violence, and exploitative wealth that run like threads through the fabric of the history of the United States. For all of the examples in which religion undergirded violence or oppression, still some stories tell of alternatives that have embraced peace, service, mutual aid, and a critique of amassing wealth. The stories suggested here form a patchwork, not a continuous chain connecting all of these groups and people. However, from this patchwork comes a picture of what Christian resistance to power and disparate wealth has looked like at times in the past. These stories form a context in which Christians continue to ask in the present how faith makes a difference in the public practice of faith and discipleship.

NOTES

[1] James C. Juhnke and Carol M. Hunter, *The Missing Peace: The Search for Nonviolent Alternatives in United States History*, 2nd exp. ed. (Kitchener, Ontario: Pandora Press, 2004), 9–16. This book provides a much fuller account of the issues raised here, and it is essential reading for anyone interested in these questions.

[2] Mark A. Noll, *A History of Christianity in the United States and Canada* (Grand Rapids, MI: Wm. B. Eerdmans, 1992), 56–60.

[3] Ibid., 26–29.

[4] Peter Brock, *The Quaker Peace Testimony, 1660 to 1914* (York, England: Sessions Book Trust, 1990), 87–115, 124–125.

[5] Juhnke and Hunter, *The Missing Peace*, 55–78. Also essential is Peter Brock, *Pacifism in the United States from the Colonial Era to the First World War* (Princeton, NJ: Princeton University Press, 1968); and Peter Brock and Nigel Young, *Pacifism in the Twentieth Century* (Syracuse, NY: Syracuse University Press, 1999).

[6] Kenneth G. Hamilton and J. Taylor Hamilton, *History of the Moravian Church: The Renewed Unitas Fratrum, 1722–1957* (Bethlehem, PA: Interprovincial Board of Christian Education, Moravian Church in America, 1967), 225–228, 233, 282.

[7] For a brief review of the Hutterites and some comments on the Bruderhof communities, see Gertrude E. Huntington, "Living in the Ark: Four Centuries of Hutterite Faith and Community," in *America's Communal Utopias*, ed. Donald E. Pitzer, 319–351 (Chapel Hill: University of North Carolina Press, 1997). The Hutterites began in 1528 as a collection of various Anabaptist refugees. Jakob Hutter organized their communal patterns and became their first leader (*Vorsteher*) in 1533.

[8] Leo Driedger and Donald B. Kraybill, *Mennonite Peacemaking: From Quietism to Activism* (Scottdale, PA: Herald Press, 1994), 165.

[9] Noll, *History of Christianity*, 386–388.

[10] Anne Klejment and Nancy L. Roberts, eds., *American Catholic Pacifism: The Influence of Dorothy Day and the Catholic Worker Movement* (Westport, CT: Praeger, 1996), 1–9, 15–32.

[11] Eileen Egan, "The Struggle of Pax," in Klejment and Roberts, *American Catholic Pacifism*, 123–128, 146–148. Egan points out that the Catholic Association for International Peace (CAIP), founded in 1927, a group involving the hierarchy of American Catholics, upheld more traditional just-war views (124).

[12] J. Kenneth Kreider, *A Cup of Cold Water: The Story of Brethren Service* (Elgin, IL: Brethren Press, 2001), 18.

[13] Hamilton and Hamilton, *History of the Moravian Church*, 82–93.

[14] Juhnke and Hunter, *The Missing Peace*, 79–83.

[15] There is still some controversy about how to interpret the religious identity of the immigrants from the German city of Krefeld who founded Germantown in 1683. Many of them had Mennonite backgrounds but associated with the Quakers in Krefeld. By 1708 there were some Mennonites who wanted to claim their separate identity to the point of forming a Mennonite congregation. See Richard McMaster, *Land, Piety, Peoplehood: The Establishment of Mennonite Communities in America, 1683–1790* (Scottdale, PA: Herald Press, 1985), 34–49.

[16] Ibid., 101.

[17] Donald F. Durnbaugh, ed., *The Brethren in Colonial America* (Elgin, IL: Brethren Press, 1967), 207–209.

[18] Juhnke and Hunter, *The Missing Peace*, 87, 94, 100.

[19] James Oliver Horton and Lois E. Horton, *Slavery and the Making of America* (New York: Oxford University Press, 2005), 74–77, 129–139, 144–146.

[20] Philip A. Klinkner and Rogers A. Smith, *The Unsteady March: The Rise and Decline of Racial Equality in America* (Chicago: University of Chicago Press, 1999), 95–105.

[21] Ibid., 107–113.

[22] Donald E. Pitzer, ed., *America's Communal Utopias* (Chapel Hill: University of North Carolina Press, 1997), 14–26; Jeff Bach, *Voices of the Turtledoves: The Sacred World of Ephrata* (University Park, PA: Penn State Press, 2003), 30–43, 97–114.

[23] Stephen J. Stein, *The Shaker Experience in America* (New Haven, CT: Yale University Press, 1992), 2–49. Another version of

their formal name is The United Society of Believers in Christ's Second Appearing.

[24] Pitzer, *America's Communal Utopias*, 57–87.

[25] Peter Hoehnle, *The Amana People: The History of a Religious Community* (Iowa City, IA: Penfield Books, 2003), 17–40.

[26] Donald B. Kraybill, *The Riddle of Amish Culture*, 2nd ed. (Baltimore: Johns Hopkins University Press, 2001), 101–106, 238–258; see also Donald B. Kraybill and Steven M. Nolt, *Amish Enterprise: From Plows to Profits*, 2nd ed. (Baltimore: Johns Hopkins University Press, 2004), 36–172.

[27] Jack S. Blocker Jr., *American Temperance Movements: Cycles of Reform* (Boston: Twayne Publishers, 1989), 8–11, 15–16, 81–85, 100–111.

[28] Felix Reichmann and Eugene Doll, *Ephrata as Seen by Contemporaries* (Allentown, PA: Schlechter's, 1953), 3, 73; Friedsam Gottrecht, *Deliciae Ephratenses,* Part 1, *Geistliche Reden* (Ephrata, PA: Typis Societatis), 10–11.

[29] Kreider, *A Cup of Cold Water*, 4–10; Driedger and Kraybill, *Mennonite Peacemaking*, 62–70.

[30] Kreider, *A Cup of Cold Water*, 399–401.

[31] Noll, *History of Christianity*, 464–469, 488–494, 532–536.

PART 2
PRAYERS AND POSSIBILITIES
FOR CHRISTIAN RESISTANCE
TODAY

We Pray for the Courage to Resist

Alison L. Boden

Our gracious God, Source and End of all
     we cherish,
we pray for courage and we pray for faith.
In every time, those who have sought
to follow the Way of Jesus Christ
have found the path to be challenging,
and so do we.
We are in the world of empire
but wish to be not of it.
We enjoy to the fullest
the large and small benefits of power,
knowing that we may forfeit some
as we work to share power with others.
We love our families,
we love our country,
we love your world,
we pray for ourselves.
That we may love and serve with integrity,
     send us your Spirit!

We pray, great God, for the courage to
    resist—
to resist inner voices of fear and of selfish-
    ness
that make us hoard what privilege we have;
to resist policies and structures that mask
violence, hatred, greed, or discrimination;
to resist those who proclaim
that dominations cannot end
nor can justice come to all.
Grant us the courage to risk,
the courage to suffer,
the courage to choose well
the direction of our days.
That we may have the courage to resist,
    send us your Spirit!

We pray, gracious God, for the faith to
    resist—
to speak truth to power,
be ministers of reconciliation,
and builders of your beloved community.
Grant us the wisdom that is born of faith,
discerning the spirits,
naming the devious,
proclaiming your truth.
Filled with your love
that will not let us go,
may we be empowered to love in return
all people around us
and those we may never come to know.
May we see you, great God, in them,
thou source of human dignity.
Grant us the faith to be the disciples you
    need
even here, even now.

That we may have the faith to resist, send
    us your Spirit!

Send us your Spirit of resistance, O God,
lest we make our peace with the suffering
    of others,
lest we lower our commitments and call it
    progress,
lest we be silent in the face of oppression,
lest we not testify with the whole of our
    lives to your inbreaking realm,
on earth as it is in heaven.

In the name of Christ we pray. Amen.

Resisting Religion,
Spreading Love

William L. (Scotty) McLennan

Remember those Gospel passages so often quoted to create the image of a meek and mild Jesus? "Do not resist an evil doer. But if anyone strikes you on the right cheek, turn the other also" (Mt 5:39). "Blessed are the peacemakers, for they will be called children of God" (Mt 5:9). "Love your enemies and pray for those who persecute you" (Mt 5:44). By contrast, there's a Gospel passage in John 2:13–22 where Jesus fashions a whip and violently drives people out of the Temple in Jerusalem, along with the sheep and cattle they're selling for ritual sacrifices. He also violently overturns the tables of moneychangers and pours out all of their coins. This incident is repeated in some form or another in all four of the Gospels: Matthew, Mark, Luke, and John.

The story of Jesus in the Temple has inspired great minds through the years, and there's even a striking painting by El Greco that has Jesus flailing away with his whip at cowering moneychangers. Significantly, though, the passage does not stand alone. There are other passages in the New Testament where Jesus insists that "the one who has no sword must sell his cloak and buy one" (Lk 22:36, 38), and where he exclaims, "I have come not to bring peace, but a sword" (Mt 10:34). That's surprising news for those of us accustomed to the meek and mild Jesus. We're just not used to Jesus the Violent.

Let's get the setting of the John 2 passage right. In Israel at that time there was only one temple, and it was located in the ancient capital of Jerusalem. The action we're considering took place around 30 C.E., but John, writing some fifty years later, knew that after a thousand years of history, the Temple had been utterly destroyed by the Romans in 70 C.E. Yet at the time the Jewish Jesus is living, the Temple is being reconstructed and its priests are at the height of their power as official leaders of Judaism. Jesus is a country bumpkin from the Galilee region, recently arrived in the big city. In three of the four Gospel accounts (Matthew, Mark, and Luke), going to the Temple is the first thing Jesus does after his triumphal arrival in Jerusalem less than a week before he's killed. It appears to be precisely because of this brash, violent act in the Temple that he's targeted for execution, for this was a deep offense to the religious authorities in Jerusalem. As the Gospel of Mark puts it, "When the chief priests and the scribes heard it, they kept looking for a way to kill him" (11:18). Perhaps Jesus should have heeded his own words about violence breeding violence: "All who take the sword will perish by the sword" (Mt 26:52).

Now why were all these sheep, cattle, and doves being sold inside the Temple in the first place, and what were the moneychangers doing there? Pilgrims were coming from all over the region for the Passover holiday, and animal sacrifice was central to religious practice in the Temple. Rather than the faithful undergoing the expense of bringing cows, sheep, and birds with them from afar, animals that could become burnt offerings were on sale right at the Temple when they arrived. However, the normal Roman currency couldn't be used for purchase, because of the idolatry of having a graven image of the supposedly divine Caesar on it. Therefore, as a service to the pilgrims, moneychangers exchanged the Roman coins for shekels, which could then be used as tender for the sacrificial animals.

According to the account in John, Jesus doesn't seem concerned with the possible dishonesty of the traffickers in the Temple. There's nothing about the den of thieves mentioned in the other Gospels. Instead, he's concerned with the system of sacrifice itself and the whole temple cult. When he says "Destroy this temple, and in three days I will raise it up" (John 2:19), he's referring to himself as the good news that will replace the temple cult.

In his book on Jesus, Catholic historian and social critic Garry Wills explains that "the most striking, resented, and dangerous of Jesus' activities was his opposition to religion as that was understood in his time. This is what led to his death. Religion killed him."[1] It begins with Jesus' rejection of animal sacrifice. As he says a couple of times, "Go and learn what this means, 'I desire mercy, not sacrifice'" (Mt 9:13). He's referring to words of the prophet Hosea, speaking for God, in the Hebrew scriptures: "Hear this, O priests! . . . I desire mercy and steadfast love, not sacrifice; the knowledge of God rather than burnt offerings" (Hos 5:1, 6:6). At another point Jesus commends a religious official who says that "To love God with one's entire heart, mind and strength, and to love one's neighbor as oneself—that is much more important than any kind of burnt offering or sacrifice" (Mk 12:33).

Jesus then moves on to challenge the priesthood itself. As he tells the parable of the Good Samaritan to illustrate how to love one's neighbor as oneself, it's a priest on the way from Jerusalem to Jericho who first passes by the robbed, stripped, and beaten man, leaving him unassisted on the side of the road. It's priests who are constantly portrayed as Jesus' mortal enemies. Not a single priest is cited as being among his followers.

Finally, Jesus questions the importance of the Temple itself to the spiritual life: "Destroy this temple and in three days I will raise it up." The temple cult is to be replaced by Jesus' inner religion, centered in himself as the embodiment of God's love. Garry Wills wonders what Jesus today would think of Saint Peter's Basilica in Rome, the Mormon Tabernacle in Salt Lake City, or Robert Schuller's Crystal Cathedral in Garden Grove, California. "Jesus did not come to replace the Temple with other buildings, whether huts or rich cathedrals," Wills states, "but to instill a religion of the heart."[2] Of course, we also might wonder what Jesus would think of the Stanford Memorial Church and its vested clergy—including me.

What might the image of Jesus with a whip in the Temple tell us about institutional religion in our time—in particular about Christian churches, clergy, and practice? First, there's the specter of a nine-hundred-foot-tall Jesus telling Oral Roberts in 1980 to build his City of Faith with three skyscrapers in Tulsa, Oklahoma, and then in 1987, during a television fundraising drive, of Roberts announcing that God had warned that he'd "call him home" unless Roberts raised enough money by March.[3] Is that really what Jesus is doing with his whip in this era? Scholar Michael True has stated of the twentieth-century figure Dorothy Day, founder of the Catholic Worker Movement in America and one who was personally committed to voluntary poverty: "I don't think the [church] hierarchy quite knew what to do with her. She was like having a time bomb in your diocese because she might tell all. She could see the scandal, see all the rich properties owned by the church. So she's one of those people who's much easier to applaud now that she's dead."[4]

As for clergy, Jesus condemned religious leaders of his day who looked righteous on the outside but inside were "full of greed and self-indulgence" (Mt 28:25). We might remember, for example, Pat Robertson's protege Jim Bakker, who started his own enormously successful televangelism empire and Heritage USA theme park with his wife, Tammy Faye. His personal compensation in the mid-1980s reached well over a million dollars a year, and the Bakkers owned a house in Palm

Springs, four condominiums in other parts of California, and a Rolls Royce. In the late 1980s, though, Bakker was found to be having an affair with his former secretary and then imprisoned after a federal conviction on fraud charges for financial irregularities in his PTL (Praise the Lord) organization. Of course, sex scandals have affected many other Protestant clergy and Roman Catholic priests, and these scandals, along with financial improprieties, have led clergy to plummet in professional-trustworthiness polls by the Gallup organization to the lowest point ever by 2003, with only 52 percent of Americans giving my profession high marks.[5]

Finally, there's religious practice in our day. We're not doing a lot of animal sacrifice in churches any more, but Jesus stressed love of God and love of neighbor as central religious duties. He constantly crossed lines of ritual purity to be with those considered unclean—lepers, the insane, prostitutes, adulterers, and collaborators with Rome. Garry Wills asks who the outcasts and cursed of our day are—with whom Jesus would be quick to align himself in love. "Gays and lesbians," is Wills's answer. He writes about Christian groups that carry placards saying "God hates fags" at the funerals of gay men who died of AIDS—and about Christian burials being denied to openly gay men. As Wills puts it, "Is there any doubt where Jesus would have stood in these episodes? . . . He was with the gay man, not with his haters. This is made all the clearer by the fact that gays are called unclean for the same reason as were other outcasts of Jesus' time—because they violate the Holiness Code of the Book of Leviticus."[6]

There's a tongue-in-cheek letter circulating widely on the Internet, addressed to a Christian (whom it is addressed to depends on the poster's agenda) who's assumed to take everything in the Holiness Code as seriously as the two lines in Leviticus (18:22 and 20:13) that say that it's an abomination for a man to lie with a male as with a woman. The amusing letter reads, "Leviticus 25:44 states that I may possess slaves, both male and female, provided they are purchased from neighboring nations. A friend of mine claims that this applies to Mexicans but not Canadians. Can you clarify? . . . I have a neighbor who insists on working on the Sabbath. Exodus 35:2 clearly states that he should be put to death. Am I morally obliged to kill him myself, or should I ask the police to do it? . . . I know from Leviticus 11:8 that touching the skin of a dead pig makes me unclean, but may I still play football if I wear gloves?" And the letter goes on in this vein to ask seven more questions. How much patience do you think Jesus in the Temple with his whip would have with these kinds of questions?

So what do we make of Jesus the Violent? What of the Jesus who thunders, "Woe to you, scribes and Pharisees, hypocrites! . . . For you are like whitewashed tombs, which on the outside look beautiful, but inside they are full of the bones of the dead and all kinds of filth. . . . You testify against yourselves that you are descendants of those who murdered the prophets. . . . You snakes, you brood of vipers! How can you escape being sentenced to hell?" (Mt 23:25–33). I agree with Wills that there's no doubt that Jesus was opposed to war and violence. "More than any other teacher of nonviolence—more than Thoreau, than Gandhi, than Dr. King"—love was the test for him. "In the gospel of Jesus," Wills adds, "love is everything." So this action in the Temple was really a "breathtaking explosion of a man not easily aroused."[7] This was highly unusual behavior for Jesus.

What exactly stimulates this level of righteous indignation? Institutional religion gone wrong—that's what. Clergy pursuing religious practices that have gone far astray from what's really important. A huge, glorious temple dedicated to an abomination rather than to love of God and neighbor.

Jesus roars in the tradition of the prophet Isaiah:

> Hear the word of the LORD . . .
> What to me is the multitude of your
>   sacrifices? . . .

> I have had enough of burnt-offerings of
>   rams . . .
>
>   who asked this from your hand?
>   Trample my courts no more;
> bringing offerings is futile;
>   incense is an abomination to me. . . .
> Cease to do evil,
>   learn to do good;
> seek justice,
>   rescue the oppressed,
> defend the orphan,
>   plead for the widow. (Is 1:10–17)

Jesus cries out in the tradition of the prophet Micah:

> With what shall I come before the LORD? . . .
> Shall I come before him with burnt-offer-
>   ings;
>   with calves a year old? . . .
> He has told you, O mortal, what is good;
>   and what does the LORD require of you
> but to do justice, and to love kindness,
>   and to walk humbly with your God?
>   (Mic 6:6–8)

So let's hope the nonviolent Jesus didn't badly hurt anyone as he drove the moneychangers and their animals out of the Temple with his whip and overturned their tables. He paid for his anger in the Temple with his own life. But he'd come to the very center of his religious tradition and found it totally misdirected. "Turn back, turn back," he'd cried, and put a little muscle behind it. Might we listen and respond in our own time to the visionary dream that earth might be fair and all its people one.[8]

NOTES

[1] Garry Wills, *What Jesus Meant* (New York: Viking, 2006), 59.

[2] Ibid., 75–76.

[3] Quoted at "Oral Roberts," http://en.wikipedia.org/wiki/Oral_Roberts.

[4] Michael True, professor emeritus of Assumption College, Worchester, Massachusetts, as quoted in Rosalie G. Riegle, *Dorothy Day: Portraits by Those Who Knew Her* (Maryknoll, NY: Orbis Books, 2003), 94.

[5] Religion News Service, "Clergy Ratings at Lowest Point Ever," *Christianity Today* (February 2003), 21.

[6] Wills, *What Jesus Meant,* 32.

[7] Ibid., 52, 56, 24.

[8] Clifford Bax, "Turn Back," Hymn 120, in *Singing the Living Tradition* (Boston: Beacon Press, 1993).

Make Us Disciples
of a More Excellent Way

Tracy Wenger Sadd

Eternal Spirit of the Universe,
Ancient of Days,
Thou who art
    the source of all true religion
    and the ultimate mystery beyond all
      religions,
Save us from religion that
    builds boundaries where they ought not
      to be
    aligns itself with empire
    hardens into fundamentalism
    fabricates idolatry
    promotes partisanship
    endorses—and even induces—violence
    yields propaganda
    and paralyzes
      with its soul-killing legalism.

Living God
    Who abhors burnt offerings and sacrifices

Who cannot be controlled by superstitious acts
Whose name is I AM WHO I AM,
We confess
our addiction
to absolutes, static dogmas,
outward forms
and our discomfort
with ambiguity, vulnerability,
the "other."

Trinitarian God
Who art relationship in thy very being
Reconnect us to the true center that will
hold.
Make us
not devotees
of institutions, ideologies, or specific
rites,
but rather disciples
of a more excellent way.
Free us from false devotion
even to the creed of resistance—
that we might be saved from giving
power
to the things we resist
in making them
the focus of our energy.
Liberate us from humanistic religion
that worships at the altars
of intellect, intention, and will.
Open us to our full humanity.
Inspire us to seek
what the great human souls have
sought.
Remind us that in genuine religion is found

Reverence and awe
Wonder and worship
Love of mystery
Humilty and humor
Compassion and community
Tolerance of paradox
Peace that passes all understanding.

Lord God,
Grant us thy Holy Spirit—the authentic
        breath of life
Create in us a faith
    that brings both life abundant
        and a deep conviction
            that we are citizens of a new age,
                when it shall be on earth
                    as it is in heaven.

May thy church be the faithful sanctuary
        For the hopes and fears of all humanity
            Now and forevermore.
                Amen.

Resisting Violence, Creating Peace

Jack Nelson-Pallmeyer

Jesus encouraged his friends and followers to reject violence and become peacemakers. Good advice then and now. Unfortunately, good advice is often rejected. Oppression and violence permeated Palestine in the first century, and violent expectations of God and history dominated the hopes and views of most of Jesus' contemporaries. They were unable fully to embrace his vision. We face similar difficulties. Many people believe that human- or God-inflicted violence is the key to earthly or end-time justice. Few believe peace is possible, and fewer still believe that peace can be achieved without using violent means. Violence so pervades our culture, theology, foreign policy, and expectations that it has become, in Walter Wink's apt phrase, "the real religion of America."[1]

A more peaceful world is possible. That is our hope. Violence is an obstacle to peace. That is our challenge. Resisting violence, therefore, is a practical and theological necessity as we seek to create a more peaceful world.

MY INTRODUCTION TO THE SPIRAL OF VIOLENCE

My student group from St. Olaf College arrived in Israel in 1972 the day after the "Munich massacre." Terrorists connected to the Palestinian group Black September had taken members of the Israeli Olympic team hostage, and eleven athletes and coaches had been killed during a raid to free them. The atmosphere in Israel upon our arrival was tense, with people expressing a mixture of sadness, fear, and rage. Israel's response to the tragedy in Munich included Operation Wrath of God, with air strikes and assassinations of those it held responsible for planning the terrorist actions. I remember our tour guide teaching us folk songs while Israeli jets flew overhead and dropped bombs on nearby Palestinian refugee camps. This led, predictably, to further attacks by Palestinians.

I knew little about the conflict. What was clear was that Israelis and Palestinians believed they were justified in using violence against the other and that their use of violence would be effective. One act of violence led to another, and it was and is hard to see how this could possibly lead to peace.

Years later, when I studied liberation theology with Gustavo Gutiérrez at Union Theological Seminary, I realized that in Israel I had witnessed a spiral of violence. The violence of the Israeli occupation of Palestinian lands triggered terrorist actions in Munich that led to retaliation by Israel. This cycle repeated itself with increasingly deadly results.

Liberation theology describes a spiral of violence with three key dimensions or spokes.[2] Violence #1 is characterized by oppression, hunger, and poverty. Children who die of hunger or who are stunted by malnutrition are victims of violence. So too are people whose ill health, illiteracy, and death are linked to unjust economic systems. Liberation theology speaks of institutionalized violence and social sin in order to highlight that violence #1 is rooted in the structures of an unjust situation or society.

Violence #2, the second spoke in the spiral, is characterized by rebellion. It is a response to and predictable outcome of violence #1. People living and dying amid poverty, social injustice, or oppression sometimes use violent means to resist. Violent rebellion often marks an escalation in a conflict after peaceful protests seem to have failed. It is often considered an option of "last resort" after other methods of protest have been ignored, rejected, or violently crushed.

Violence #3, according to liberation theology, is the repressive violence used by powerful groups to put down rebellions. This includes the lethal violence of military forces aligned with the state and economic elites, and the terror and torture practices of paramilitary groups and death squads associated with them. Most rebellions are violently suppressed because the resources and lethal violence of the state and its allies are generally far superior to those of protesters and insurgents. State violence and terror (#3) can successfully, though sometimes only temporarily, crush violent rebellions (#2). They often deepen the violence of hunger, poverty, oppression, and social inequality (#1). As social injustices worsen, new protests arise, and without substantive changes, another round of rebellion and repression follows. The spiral of violence intensifies.

My second introduction to the spiral of violence was in Bombay, India, in 1972. My group got on a bus at the Bombay airport and headed toward downtown. It was late, and along the way we witnessed many thousands of people getting ready for bed—only they didn't have homes, and they didn't have beds. I felt as if I was driving through the "bedrooms" of an entire city as I watched people place a piece of cardboard, a cloth, or a mat on the ground between the roadways.

The bus stopped, and I looked out the window to see a woman who was dead and a little girl next to her screaming. After what seemed an eternity, the bus lurched forward and we arrived at a luxury hotel amid squalor. We were ushered into the hotel by armed guards, and awaiting us was a feast complete with fine china and an orchestra. I didn't want to eat or stay there. I pushed past the guards onto the street and spent much of the night walking.

I remember thinking that night that a luxury hotel with armed guards amid poverty was a disturbing metaphor for our world. I was outraged by that world, and I made a commitment that night to work to change it. Unknowingly, I had once again been confronted by a spiral of violence. In this case, I witnessed unimaginable poverty in Bombay (violence #1), the fear that poor people might rebel (violence #2), and armed guards capable of repressing the poor (violence #3) in order to maintain present inequalities and injustices.

Our challenge is to break the spiral of violence in order to create a more peaceful world. Doing so requires that we resist and reject violence in each of these spokes and in all of its forms.

A PARABLE FROM JESUS

Oppressive systems require resistance. But how are we to resist? Violence is seductive. Powerful groups use violence to maintain unjust systems, and oppressed people use violent means in an effort to change their situation for the better. Peace seems illusive. Achieving peace without recourse to violence seems unrealistic. Faced with grave injustices, violence is a tempting option even if it is unlikely to achieve desired changes.

Jesus critiqued and discouraged violent resistance to oppression in a parable whose social setting mirrored that of many of his contemporaries in rural Galilee. Peasants had always paid an outrageous percentage of their crops to taxes and tithes, but during Roman rule they were losing their land due to debt. The wealthy absentee owners who replaced them often planted vineyards to raise grapes that could be turned into wine, an exportable commodity. Jesus told the following parable in order to expose deadly dynamics in the oppressive system, including the futility of violence:

> Then he began to speak to them in parables. "A man planted a vineyard, put a fence around it, dug a pit for

the wine press, and built a watchtower; then he leased it to tenants and went to another country. When the season came, he sent a slave to the tenants to collect from them his share of the produce of the vineyard. But they seized him, and beat him, and sent him away empty-handed. And again he sent another slave to them; this one they beat over the head and insulted. Then he sent another, and that one they killed. And so it was with many others; some they beat, and others they killed. He had still one other, a beloved son. Finally he sent him to them, saying, 'They will respect my son.' But those tenants said to one another, 'This is the heir; come, let us kill him, and the inheritance will be ours.' So they seized him, killed him, and threw him out of the vineyard. What then will the owner of the vineyard do? He will come and destroy the tenants and give the vineyard to others." (Mk 12:1–9)

This parable is often interpreted as a story about wicked tenants. Mark theologized its meaning, and in doing so turned an oppressive absentee owner into a God figure. Mark and interpreters who follow his lead aren't interested in what Jesus meant in the context of the oppressive system of first-century Palestine. Rather, they seek to explain why Jesus was rejected and eventually killed and to demonstrate that his rejection fulfilled God's promises, as recorded in the Hebrew scriptures. Mark places a scriptural quotation on Jesus' lips: "The stone that the builders rejected has become the cornerstone; this was the Lord's doing, and it is amazing in our eyes" (v. 10). William Herzog describes the parable's meaning for Mark and most interpreters:

The man who planted the vineyard is Yahweh, and the vineyard itself refers to Israel whether as a historical manifestation of God's people or as God's kingdom. . . . The tenants are the leaders of Israel, specifically, the

Jerusalem authorities; the servants are the prophets sent
by God; and the "beloved son" . . . is Jesus himself, the
culminating messenger and servant. . . . "The others"
refers to the emerging church as the new vineyard of
God whose leaders will become the new tenants of the
vineyard.[3]

Herzog believes we should look at this and other parables
differently. "Parables," he writes, "were not earthly stories
with heavenly meanings but earthy stories with heavy meanings." Parables shed light on "the reigning systems of oppression."[4] He renames this parable "Peasant Revolt and the Spiral of Violence."[5] Peasants in first-century Palestine resented
wealthy landowners who pushed them off their ancestral lands
and converted their lands into vineyards. Displaced peasants
were hired to work their former lands as tenants raising the
new owner's export crop. With their survival at stake, rebellion may have seemed the only option. As the parable unfolds, one senses the exhilaration of the oppressed tenants
and those living vicariously through its telling. The humili-
ated humiliate others. The shamed do the shaming. The ones
often killed or considered disposable kill and dispose of the
body of the owner's son. The disinherited, and rightful, heirs
to the land deny the inheritance of an illegitimate heir. There
must have been a feeling of power as oppression gave way to
rebellion and the vicarious experience of justified revenge.

Had the parable ended there, Jesus' hearers may have joined
together and gone on a rampage against any deserving oppressor. But Jesus' parable included an ominous question and
response: "What then will the owner of the vineyard do? He
will come and destroy the tenants and give the vineyard to
others." The parable highlights the spiral of violence, under-
scores the futility of violent rebellion, and leaves one groping
for alternative forms of protest and resistance.

This reading of the parable is consistent with other aspects of Jesus' life and teaching. Against a backdrop of common wisdom in which salvation was equated with defeat of

enemies, Jesus taught love of enemies because it is the very nature of God to bless all (Mt 5:43–45). Jesus went beyond love of enemies. He shocked his listeners with a pointed parable suggesting we are saved by our enemies. It was a compassionate Samaritan (Samaritans were despised), after all, who saved a beaten Jew (Lk 10:4). Jesus also rejected the common apocalyptic expectation that hope resides at an end-time vindication ushered in by God's violent judgment in favor of the daily presence of God within (Lk 17:20–21). He blessed the peacemakers (Mt 5:9) and modeled nonviolent action in the face of injustice:

> You have heard that it was said, "An eye for an eye and a tooth for a tooth." But I say to you, Do not resist an evildoer. But if anyone strikes you on the right cheek, turn the other also; and if anyone wants to sue you and take your coat, give your cloak as well; and if anyone forces you to go one mile, go also the second mile. Give to everyone who begs from you, and do not refuse anyone who wants to borrow from you. (Mt 5:38–42)

According to Walter Wink, Jesus modeled an alternative to "two deeply instinctual responses to violence: flight or fight." "Jesus," Wink writes, "offers a third way: nonviolent direct action."[6] In order to understand what Jesus advocated, we need to clarify one word and examine the three examples he offers (turn other cheek, give cloak, walk extra mile). The Greek word *anthistémi*, translated above as "resist," is used most often as a military term. It refers to violent struggle or resistance in military encounters.[7] The translation would more accurately read "do not violently resist an evildoer." The Jesus Seminar captures the essence of this verse perfectly: "Don't react violently against the one who is evil."[8]

Jesus offered exploited people in Palestine three examples of creative nonviolent resistance to oppression. Slapping, suing, and forcing imply that someone with power is taking advantage of others who are vulnerable. The question in each,

Wink notes, "is how the oppressed can recover the initiative and assert their human dignity in a situation that cannot for the time being be changed."[9] Humiliation was and is a fact of daily life for oppressed people. A backhand slap admonished inferiors. As Wink notes, turning the other cheek was a way of saying: "Try again. Your first blow failed to achieve its intended effect. I deny you the power to humiliate me. I am a human being just like you. Your status does not alter that fact. You cannot demean me."[10]

We see similar dynamics in the other nonviolent actions encouraged by Jesus. If they threaten to sue you and take your outer garment (they have probably already stolen your land), then give them your underwear. Stand naked before the court, shame the system, and humiliate all who look upon you. If a Roman soldier forces you to carry his pack the legally prescribed one mile (forcing someone to go further is against the law), then keep going and throw your oppressor off balance. This may not constitute a dramatic victory, but it is something. And as Wink notes, it "is in the context of Roman military occupation that Jesus speaks" and with full awareness "of the futility of armed insurrection against Roman imperial might."[11] Similar tactics were successfully employed by Gandhi and Martin Luther King Jr. and their followers to defeat the British Empire and achieve civil rights in the United States.

The concrete examples of creative nonviolence offered by Jesus demonstrate that he rejected violence as a means to peace. He also rejected messianic and apocalyptic fantasies that linked the defeat, destruction, or overturning of oppressive conditions to future violent acts of God. We are called to resist violence and create peace. This is our vocation as people of faith.

THREE CHALLENGES

Breaking the spiral of violence will require us to face three important challenges. The first is fully to commit ourselves to resisting violence by ending hunger and poverty. The world is fracturing under the weight of unimaginable inequalities. Nearly half the world's people are trying to live on less than two dollars a day, and the three richest people have assets that exceed the combined gross domestic product of the forty-eight poorest countries. As a United Nations report on human development states, "Global inequalities in income and living standards have reached grotesque proportions."[12] At the Franklin Delano Roosevelt memorial in Washington DC the following quotation from FDR is etched in granite: "Unless the peace that is coming recognizes that the whole world is one neighborhood and does justice to the whole human race then the germs of another world war will remain a constant threat."

By lessening hunger and poverty (violence #1), we diminish social unrest that triggers resentment and rebellion (violence #2) and eliminate the defense of injustice through repression (violence #3). Greater justice, in other words, is the key to resisting violence and creating peace. Environmentalist Lester Brown lays out an "eradicating poverty initiative" that would lessen violence by meeting the following basic social goals worldwide: universal primary education, adult literacy, school lunch programs and assistance to preschool children and pregnant women in the forty-four poorest countries, reproductive health and family planning, and universal health care. To achieve these goals will require additional yearly expenditures of $68 billion (less than 10 percent of projected U.S. military spending in 2008).

Brown also describes "earth restoration goals," including reforesting the earth, protecting topsoil on cropland, restoring rangelands, stabilizing water tables, restoring fisheries, and protecting biological diversity. The price tag is modest, additional yearly expenditures of $93 billion. The cumulative cost of eradicating poverty and restoring ecological balance is $161 billion a year. This cost, which could be borne by many nations, is about one-fourth of projected U.S. military spending in 2008. Or, consider that annual subsidies worldwide for fossil fuels are estimated to be $210 billion. Ending poverty and restoring the earth are realistic, practical, and necessary goals. We cannot afford to miss this opportunity or fail to accept this challenge. Brown writes:

> It is hard to find words to convey the gravity of our situation and the momentous nature of the decision we are about to make. How can we convey the urgency of this moment in history? Will tomorrow be too late? Do enough of us care deeply enough to turn the tide now? Will someone one day erect a tombstone for our civilization? If so, what will it read? It cannot say we did not understand. We do understand. It cannot say we did not have the resources. We do have the resources. It can only say we were too slow to respond to the forces undermining our civilization. Time ran out.[13]

Our second core challenge if we are to resist violence and create peace is to address climate change and build a truly sustainable economy. James Hanson, lead environmental scientist at NASA, wrote in 2006 that "we have at most ten years" to make fundamental changes. "Our children, grandchildren, and many more generations will bear the consequences of choices that we make in the next few years." More hopefully, he noted: "It's not too late. [A positive] outcome is still feasible in the case of global warming, but just barely."[14] If we are to resist violence and create peace, as U.S. citizens we must chart a radically different course for our nation. We must demonstrate that a resource-wasteful, oil-dependent nation can transition to a sustainable society within a very short time.

Unfortunately, U.S. leaders have a very different agenda. For example, the Bush administration, with the complicity of many Democrats, invaded and continues to occupy Iraq. It was part of what the neoconservatives called "America's grand strategy" to turn present military superiority into permanent global domination. Stealing Iraqi oil and establishing permanent military bases were key objectives of the invasion and occupation.[15] Confronted with the folly of the neoconservative ambition, a Bush senior aide dismissed critics: "We're an empire now," he said prior to the invasion, "and when we act, we create our own reality."[16]

Iraq is a disaster, but the problem is deeper. The United States is poised to borrow nearly $10 trillion to pay for imported oil over the next twenty years and fight an endless series of wars to access that oil. The alternative is to build a renewable energy economy: conserve; focus on efficiency; build windmills, solar panels, electric trains, and plug-in hybrid cars powered by renewable energy sources; retrofit existing buildings; and take other steps needed to help the world avoid resource wars and environmental disaster.

Our third urgent challenge as we seek to resist violence and create peace is to help the United States transition from empire to decent global partner. Few powerful nations have gracefully moved from a dominant role rooted in superior military power to a more modest role as world conditions changed. Most have chosen the folly of military overreach that has led to economic decline and eventual collapse. The United States is well on its way to repeating this folly. French historian Emmanuel Todd writes that for the United States, as was true for the Soviet Union (whose demise he rightly predicted), the "expansion of military activity" was seen "as a sign of increasing power when in fact it serves to mask a decline. . . . America no longer has the economic and financial resources to back up its foreign policy objectives." Huge trade deficits with the rest of the world signal that "financially speaking America has become the planet's glorious beggar." It has become the chief "predator of the globalized economy." Its "dramatic militarization" has made it "a superpower that is economically dependent but also politically useless."[17]

Present U.S. policies are internally and externally destructive. The mission in Iraq and elsewhere is exploitation, not freedom, democracy, or benevolence. One of its principal aims is to control oil and other resources. "Since a free and democratic order is slowly being sapped of its substance within the United States," Todd wrote, "the country's goal can hardly be to defend such an order abroad. From now on the fundamental strategic objective of the United States will be political control of the world's resources." The United States, he said, suffered "delusions of empire" and was on a collision course with its own delusions. Policies based on destructive military power served selective interests, but they showed weakness, not strength. And they didn't translate into effective control. U.S. "power to constrain militarily and economically is insufficient for maintaining the current levels of exploitation of the planet."[18]

According to Todd:

> The limited military, economic, and ideological resources of the United States leave it no other way of affirming its global importance than by mistreating minor powers. There is a hidden logic behind the drunken sailor appearance of American diplomacy. The real America is too weak to take on anyone except military midgets. By provoking all of these secondary players, it can at least affirm its global role. Being economically dependent on the rest of the world, it will have a global presence of one kind or another. The insufficiency of its real resources is leading to a hysterical dramatization of second-order conflicts.[19]

These are difficult words, but they must be heeded. Jesus warned that belief in the utility of violence was misplaced. The sad truth is that the United States is a military superpower but there are no military solutions to most of the problems we face. It is also true that every effort the United States makes to hold onto its superpower status through military means accelerates the pace of its internal economic decline.

As a nation we spend eighty-eight times more on war and war preparation than addressing climate change. It is also not a coincidence that the United States accounts for half of the world's military spending but has bridges falling down, an education system that fails many students, and nearly fifty million citizens without health care.

CONCLUSION

Jesus pointed out the folly of violence and called his followers to be peacemakers. Our challenge is to break the spiral of violence, resist violence, and create peace. We didn't choose it, but our choices matter because we are living in the most important decade in human history. We must help our nation redefine security and its role in the world. Doing so will allow us to lessen violence in all of its forms. We can attend to pressing domestic needs and join the community of nations to address the climate crisis, resolve conflicts peacefully, and work to end hunger and poverty. If we face these challenges with honesty and courage, this can be a hopeful time. Blessed are the peacemakers, for they shall be called children of God.

NOTES

[1] Walter Wink, *Engaging the Powers: Discernment and Resistance in a World of Domination* (Minneapolis, MN: Fortress Press, 1992), 13.

[2] See Dom Hélder Câmara, *Spiral of Violence* (London: Sheed and Ward, 1971).

[3] William R. Herzog II, *Parables as Subversive Speech: Jesus as Pedagogue of the Oppressed* (Louisville, KY: Westminster/John Knox Press, 1994), 101.

[4] Ibid., 3, 7.

[5] Ibid., chap. 6.

[6] Wink, *Engaging the Powers*, 175.

[7] Ibid., 185.

[8] Robert W. Funk, Roy W. Hoover, and The Jesus Seminar, *The Five Gospels: The Search for the Authentic Words of Jesus* (New York: Scribner, 1993), 143.

[9] Wink, *Engaging the Powers*, 182.

[10] Ibid., 176.

[11] Ibid., 181.

[12] United Nations, *Human Development Report 1999*, 104.

[13] Lester R. Brown, *Plan B 2.0: Rescuing a Planet under Stress and a Civilization in Trouble* (New York: W. W. Norton, 2006), 259.

[14] James Hansen, "The Threat to the Planet," in *The New York Review of Books* 53, no. 12 (July 13, 2006): 3.

[15] See Jack Nelson-Pallmeyer, *Saving Christianity from Empire* (New York: Continuum Books, 2005).

[16] Unidentified aide, speaking to Ron Suskind, report in "Faith, Certainty, and the Presidency of George W. Bush," *New York Times Magazine* (October 17, 2004).

[17] Emmanuel Todd, *After the Empire: The Breakdown of the American Order* (New York: Columbia University Press, 2002), xvi.

[18] Ibid., 20, 98, 77.

[19] Ibid., 132.

Help Us Be Your Peace

Stanley Hauerwas

Dear God,

You have called your people to be a people of peace in a world of war. Please help us know how to be your peace, how to work for your peace, in this time and place called America. The power of the American empire overwhelms us. Too often and too easily we are tempted to view our nation's appeal to peace as the peace of the cross. Help us see that the peace our empire offers is more often than not the same worldly power that put you on the cross. It is not your peace.

Help us to see in the midst of the American empire the subtle movements of your peace. For if we are to be your people of peace it is only this witness that will save us from self-righteousness, the self-righteousness that allows us to think we as a nation know better than others how to secure peace on earth. This same self-righteousness has blinded your church so that many of us no longer can identify the violence our nation inflicts on others because we have forgotten that only through your death and resurrection has peace been made a possibility. Dear God, we have given way to the persuasion that our violence is legitimate in your eyes because we, that is, America, know what it means to be "free." Lord, have mercy. And give us the humility born of learning to love our enemies—even when doing so poses a threat to our "security."

And save us from heroic attempts. Empires thrive on the glory of heroism. They think nothing of humble acts of charity. We pray you will give us the patience, even in the face of empire, to do, in the words of Jean Vanier, "ordinary things with tenderness." Give us the patient love to resist the temptation to confront the violence of empire on its own terms. Remind us, for we are weak, never to confuse patience with complacency. Bring into our lives those who suffer so that we might be reminded it is only on you that we can depend.

Finally, we ask that you give us courage. For it takes courage to be your people of peace. It takes courage to see empires for what they are. And it takes courage to deny empires their claim to describe us according to ungodly fear. Their thirst for power remains unquenched because the threat of limited power looms. We, your people, do not pretend to be without fears. But give us strength in the assurance that your power is without end. Through the power of your Holy Spirit help us to be the people of the resurrected Christ, the people of your peace. Amen.

Resisting Consumerism,
Building Community

Bill McKibben

Many years ago I performed an experiment, almost a piece of conceptual art. I found what was then the largest cable television system on the planet, one hundred channels. It was located in Fairfax, Virginia, and I got people there to tape for me everything that came across those hundred channels for the same twenty-four-hour period—twenty-four hundred solid hours of TV, a day in the life of the information age.

I sat for a year and watched it, trying to imagine what the world would look like if that was your main portal on it. And so, of course, one-third or so of the year was spent viewing commercials, often the same one over and over. There was one for a product called Jet-Dry, which you add to your dishwasher to remove the "invisible residue" of "food particles" left behind by the dishwasher detergent. It seemed to me a sign that we might be reaching the twilight of our high consumerism when we were reduced to buying a product to remove the undetectable remains of that dangerous compound—food—that might be adhering to our plates. I mean, we're in Lady Macbeth territory here. And yet Jet-Dry has not only survived but prospered. In fact, you can now buy it with "shine boost."

There was another ad that day, this one for Rubbermaid. Members of a family moped about their cluttered house, sombered by the realization that every horizontal space was covered with possessions. They journeyed to a store, bought a number of large plastic boxes, returned home, and secured and stacked their belongings in these crates. And then they were happy—not because the chaos of their property had been contained, but because they were now "unstuffed" and hence free to "buy more stuff." They exited the house as a happy unit, arms waving in the air, to go and buy again. It reminded me of the stories we used to tell each other as schoolboys, about how the Roman gourmands had a special room in their house, the vomitorium, to which they would repair after a number of courses in order to empty their stomachs for further repast. But at most that must have been a *few* Romans, and it sounded *gross*. This was all of us, and it sounded normal.

How did it happen? How did we turn into a people who build houses the size of junior high schools and yet still require storage lockers? The answer that the TV gave over those twenty-four hundred hours was so obvious that it's hidden in plain sight, essentially ignored as we think about our culture. Show after show, hour after hour, the TV tells each of us one over-arching thing: You are the center of the world. You are the most important thing there ever was and ever will be. In the Ptolemaic cosmology of the sofa and the remote, the universe wheels around you. It provides you with jesters and clowns, with advice, with losers to stare at in smug joy, with numberless items to make you happier or more attractive to others. And it's not just the television—the shopping mall, the theme park, the suburb itself all operate on the same principle. It's entirely about you.

In other words, the central premise of our economy is by now a kind of hyper-individualism that is, I think, relatively new to the human enterprise. Not new to us—after a couple of generations of it, we've become so deeply enmeshed that it feels to us entirely natural, normal, and obvious. Indeed, anyone who proposes a challenge of any kind to that orthodoxy is accused of idealistically going against human nature. And certainly that kind of myopia is a part of our nature, or we wouldn't respond so well to our cues—surely it's a part of our nature that every spiritual teacher we've ever revered has warned about. But never before has it been considered the *only* part of our nature. Always before humans have figured out their identity by putting something else—the tribe/community, nature, God, or some amalgam of these—near the center. Not us. We're it.

To put it in amateur theological terms: Idolatry in the old sense is not a great problem here. We're all pious; Baal worship not a great threat. But *I*-dolatry is another matter altogether.

How did it happen? Meet coal, gas, and oil. The discovery three centuries ago of how to use fossil fuel in the place of animal and human energy set the stage for all that followed, ending in the half-century crescendo of endless globalization we've just seen. Cheap energy "liberated" us in many ways—it's what allowed the West to become rich. (The average standard of living had barely doubled in all of human history before the Industrial Revolution, Keynes once estimated; now doublings take only decades). We can thank that energy for our prosperity, we can curse it (as we shall see a little later) for its effect on the health of our planet, but we should also recognize one of its most powerful effects: we became the first people on the planet who had no practical need of our neighbors. Everyone on your cul de sac could keel over tomorrow from some mysterious disease, and the effect on you might be sadness (it might not, too—three-quarters of Americans have no relationship with their next-door neighbor), but it wouldn't be starvation, the way it would have been for most people in most of human history. We depend on invisible forces acting at a great distance to bring us our shelter, clothing, food—the average calorie travels fifteen hundred miles to reach our lips in this country.

This premise—that neighbors don't count—accounts for the way we've organized our nation physically in recent times. For fifty years the American dream can be summarized like this: a bigger house, further apart from other people. In the last ruinous wave of housing construction, we found ourselves wanting to be further apart *from other members of our families;* many upscale new homes were built with dual master bedrooms so husbands and wives would have a retreat from each other's company. Solipsism Manor at Fox Run Ridge.

And this played out in our religious life as well. Look at the ways that the suburban churches and the TV pastors enticed us: financial management classes, endless shelves of books about fulfilling our potential, very little hard-to-swallow sermonizing about, you know, *others.* George Barna, the evangelical pollster, found earlier this decade that three-quarters of American Christians believed that the phrase "God helps those who help themselves" could be found in the Bible. Not only did it come from Ben Franklin instead of Jesus, it is the utter and complete opposite of the actual gospel truth—that our chief jobs are to love God and to love our neighbors as ourselves. That's what we were built for.

Which is why we need to start doing it, in effective ways that reshape our economic landscape and with it our sense of who we are. *The opposite of consumerism is not simplicity. The opposite of consumerism is community.* Simplicity may or may not help break the spell of consumerism—there are plenty of ways to consume a holier-than-thou approach to the world. You can be simple and solitary. But community by definition undermines that focus on the me that is our great distress. When sociologists followed shoppers around a farmers' market, for instance, they found that on average they had ten times as many conversations as the shoppers at a supermarket. It is a feast of connections. It brings you outside your self.

Or consider Christmas. Some years ago a few of us in the Methodist church in the Northeast began a program we called Hundred Dollar Holidays designed to change the way we celebrated Christ's birth. Pastors called on their flock to spend only a hundred dollars per family and instead to emphasize making gifts, gifts of service, time together, and so on. It was a great success in many communities, because it turns out that the holidays have become as sterile as the supermarket—polled at Thanksgiving, 75 percent of Americans view their onset more with dread than anticipation. Christmas has become an occasion to baptize consumerism—to take our youngest and most impressionable relations and tell them that this too is about them, that joy lies in getting.

And so resistance takes the form not of simplicity but of joy—a joy that almost by definition finds itself rooted in others. The percentage of Americans who consider themselves "very happy" has steadily declined in this country since the end of World War II even as our standard of living has skyrocketed. And the reason, all the data shows, is because of a perceived loss of community, of connection. We moved to the suburbs; we ran into each other less; we got a lot of screens to look at; and we now eat meals with friends and family and neighbors half as often as we did fifty years ago. We have about half as many close friends. Those are very big changes for a social animal to undergo.

Here's the interesting part, I think. This shift in the direction of community is the same shift we need to make to deal with the other great woe of our time, the ecological crisis brought on by our endless consumption of that same coal and gas and oil. The planet is heating at an unforgiving rate—instead of being stewards, we've decided to play arsonist. And why not? Until very recently it's been relatively cheap, and it's what has allowed us to live on our own individual islands. Each of us has several hundred slaves.

Dealing with that crisis one light bulb at a time is as noble as it is pointless. We need massive reductions in the amount of carbon flowing into the atmosphere. And one way to get there is to reorient our economic lives away from individual consumerism and toward the consumption of companionship, experience, community. Those farmers' markets use a lot less energy to feed us, so it's very good news that they're growing. The only part of the music industry that's growing is local live performances and festivals, the consumption of camaraderie, not CDs.

Look, if this sounds soft and ephemeral, at western Europe. There people live dignified lives, and if the statistical measures are to be trusted, they are happier with their existences than we are. But because of their commitment to community (read: high taxes for medical care, education, and so on), they have only one-half to two-thirds the private consumption that we enjoy. Not surprisingly, given that commitment to community (read: attractive cities, mass transit), they each burn half the energy on average that Americans do. Half is a big number—it's more than we're going to get from ethanol or nuclear power or anything else. It's enough to matter.

And in point of fact, it's enough to make it clear that they're better at loving their neighbors than we are. Not just their neighbors in other parts of Denmark, whom they're willing to support, but their neighbors in, say, Bangladesh. Danes aren't raising the level of the ocean and spreading malaria— we are. If we're going to change, it will require political action—require us working with our neighbors to change federal policy so that everyone pays more for carbon and hence uses it more carefully. Such a policy would spur more of the neighborliness I've described: cheap industrial food would become more expensive, making the farmers' markets more attractive, for instance. A virtuous cycle instead of the vicious one we've been living through.

We are a self-loving bunch right now. It's our ecological crime and our theological crime. And as every guru back at least as far as the Buddha has predicted, it isn't making us happy. The alternative is to love our neighbor—to build the kind of economic community that will help rebuild the human community. That's why churches need solar panels on the roof and windmills on the steeple—tied into the grid, firing electrons down the line for their neighbors. It's why churches need to be the place where, on Sunday morning, farmers deliver food for their subscription customers. It's why we need to get away from our damn selves for a while. Churches are the last big institutions in the country that can even posit some goal other than material accumulation for human existence. It's about time they did.

10

Give Us This Day Our Daily Bread

A Eucharistic Prayer

Paul Raushenbush

Sustaining God, out of our hunger for you we pray: "Give us this day our daily bread."

Responding to our need, you graciously offer us communion with your son Jesus, who in his earthly ministry provided bread for all, and who is for us the bread of life.

May we recognize in this bread your redemption for all people contained in the simplicity of grain, water, and heat. In our moment of fulfillment, help us to remember our spiritual ancestors for whom manna from heaven provided daily survival as they sojourned out of bondage into liberation.

Lord, help us to remember that your bread is for all to share so that all might live. Lead us not into the temptation of gluttonous self-satisfaction that results in the starvation of others for lack of daily bread. Relax and release the fists we have clenched around your goodness.

Calm our frenetic compulsion toward accumulation and consumption. Help us to live simply so others might simply live.

Inspire our labor so that it might yield a harvest of plenty with enough bread to sustain life throughout the world. And awaken us to your presence so that we might be present to the joys inherent in this world and see with new eyes our place within your own mighty works.

With an open hand and a thankful heart we accept this gift of bread you generously give us this day, and we commit ourselves to sharing it so that all might eat and live. Amen.

11

Resisting the Frontier, Meeting at the Border

Roberto S. Goizueta

At the beginning of his 1999 apostolic exhortation *Ecclesia in America*, Pope John Paul II challenged us to "reflect on America as a single entity." The use of the singular is appropriate, he suggested, as "an attempt to express not only the unity which in some way already exists, but also to point to that closer bond which the peoples of the continent seek and which the Church wishes to foster as part of her own mission, as she works to promote the communion of all in the Lord" (no. 5). Pope John Paul's inclusive use of the singular "America" represented both an acknowledgment of historical reality and, on the basis of such historical honesty, a call to conversion.[1] Indeed, as Cuban American theologian Justo González has observed: "What preposterous conceit allows the inhabitants of a single country to take for themselves the name of an entire hemisphere? What does this say about that country's view of those other nations who share the hemisphere with it?"[2]

The pope's challenge is today more appropriate than ever. In the Mexican War the United States conquered and annexed almost one-half of the territory of Mexico; today we are witnessing the reconquest of that territory, not by the force of arms but by the sweat of the brow, by the very power of the "American dream." In *Ecclesia in America*, Pope John Paul II challenged us to acknowledge this reality and consciously to embrace it as a source of renewal for the church in America. He challenged us to reach across geographical and cultural borders in order to embrace the rich diversity that defines our past and present, and even more, will define our future.

In the first years of this new millennium, the principal challenge confronting the Christian world is that represented by this globalization of the Christian faith. As Christianity becomes increasingly a third-world religion, shaped by the world views and cultures of those regions where the Christian faith is experiencing its greatest vitality, the future of the church will not be determined by ecclesial and theological movements in Europe. For, unlike the globalization effected through violence and conquest, this new historical reality is taking root in and being nurtured by local churches and grassroots communities. The face of this global church is marked not so much by colonization as by emigration and immigration. This global Christianity finds its cradle not in the great cathedrals of Paris and Cologne but in the poor neighborhoods of Lima, Manila, and El Paso.

It is here, in these neighborhoods, that a new church is today being born. It is here that, increasingly, Christians are looking for and encountering Jesus Christ. And in doing so they are encountering what the Mexican American theologian Virgilio Elizondo has called the *mestizo* face of Christ— and the *mestizo* face of his church. The *mestizo* is the person of mixed cultures and mixed race who is so often rejected as a "half-breed." In the person of Christ, however, this multicultural "half-breed" is the bearer—and the very embodiment—of the good news. Christ calls us to resist all borders that have become mere barriers that divide. Instead, he calls us to view borders as places of encounter between peoples.

What is more, he calls us to recognize his own liberating presence in the very midst of those encounters.

In this chapter, then, I suggest that today the border is a privileged place for encountering the gospel, a privileged locus for hearing Christ's liberating message. In order to make this argument, I first reflect on the meaning and interpretation of the very notion of the "border" in the context of U.S. history, a history marked from the beginning by a "frontier mentality." Drawing on the resources of the Gospels, as well as the popular religious practices of the Latin American people, especially that of Our Lady of Guadalupe, I then suggest the outlines of a Christian understanding of the border.

THE BORDER AS FRONTIER

In 1914 American historian Frederick Jackson Turner delivered the commencement address at the University of Washington. He ended his speech with the following lines from Tennyson's *Ulysses*:

> I am become a name
> For always roaming with an hungry heart,
> Much have I seen and known . . .
> I am a part of all that I have met;
> Yet all experience is an arch, where thro'
> Gleams that untravelled world, whose
>   margin fades
> Forever and forever when I move.
> How dull it is to pause, to make an end.
> To rust unburnished, not to shine in use!
>
> And this gray spirit yearning in desire
> To follow knowledge like a shining star
> Beyond the utmost bound of human
>   thought.

> . . . Come my friends,
> 'Tis not too late to seek a newer world.
> Push off, and sitting well in order smite
> The sounding furrows; for my purpose
>   holds
> To sail beyond the sunset, and the baths
> Of all the Western stars until I die
>
> To strive, to seek, to find and not to yield.[3]

The frontier is at the very heart of modern Western civilization, particularly as this has been exemplified in the history of the United States of America. The modern world, in this history, is constructed by forging and conquering new frontiers. "The first ideal of the pioneer," Turner wrote, "was that of conquest."[4] In his influential 1893 essay "The Significance of the Frontier in American History," Turner set forth what came to be known as the frontier thesis:

> American social development has been continually beginning over again on the frontier. This perennial rebirth, this fluidity of American life, this expansion westward with its new opportunities, its continuous touch with the simplicity of primitive society, furnish the forces dominating American character. In this advance, the frontier is the outer edge of the wave—the meeting point between savagery and civilization. . . . And now, four centuries from the discovery of America, at the end of a hundred years of life under the Constitution, the frontier has gone.[5]

By the end of the nineteenth century, the western frontier "finally closed forever, with uncertain consequences for the American future."[6]

Yet the values and world view implicit in the frontier myth, Turner argued, had already become a part of U.S. culture:

"Long after the frontier period of a particular region of the United States has passed away, the conception of society, the ideals and aspirations which it produced, persist in the minds of the people. . . . This experience has been wrought into the very warp and woof of American thought."[7] The very drive to extend the frontier had become a constitutive feature of "civilization" itself: to be civilized *is* to extend the frontier, to expand, to seek new opportunities, to dominate, to conquer (in Tennyson's words, "How dull it is to pause, to make an end"). Conversely, then, to accept limits to this expansion would be to undermine the very foundations of civilized society: "once free lands were exhausted . . . the whole moral fabric would collapse and the land descend into the state of depravity and tyranny that overcrowded Europe already knew."[8] Thus, implicit in the frontier myth is the assumption that the only alternative to expansion is decline or degeneration. This begs the question that Turner and other scholars were asking at the turn of the twentieth century: How would the United States react to the closing of the western frontier? Turner did not live to see the emergence of an answer during the remaining decades of the twentieth century.

In retrospect, however, the turn of the twentieth century represented not so much the demise of the frontier as the replacement of the western frontier with a southern frontier (or so I would suggest). Initially, this followed the pattern of military, geographical, and political expansion. Thus, in the first half of the twentieth century, the U.S. frontier became the Caribbean and Central America. The rapid growth of multinational corporations during this period provided possibilities for economic expansion unknown to earlier pioneers. When territorial expansion proved impracticable, more benign forms of economic expansion would take its place, sometimes with the aid of political and even military intervention and occupation. By the 1930s, Walter LaFeber contends, overt military intervention "had become too costly. Nor were such blatantly imperialist gestures any longer needed. The blunt instruments were replaced with the Good Neighbor's economic leverage."[9]

By 1890, U.S. Secretary of State James G. Blaine had foreseen the form that the new frontier would take, observing, "'Our great demand is expansion,' but only in trade, for 'we are not seeking annexation of territory.'"[10] Between 1898 and 1901, the United States began to export capital to a degree previously unequalled and, by World War I, had erased its trade deficits.[11] As LaFeber has argued, "The dynamic new United States necessarily prepared itself to find fresh frontiers abroad to replace the closed frontier at home." Like the earlier, westward expansion, the drive to extend the southern frontier "rested on views of history, the character of foreign peoples [that is, savagery], and politics that anticipated attitudes held by North Americans throughout much of the twentieth century. . . . North Americans seldom doubted that they could teach people to the south to act more civilized."[12]

Over a century ago Frederick Jackson Turner observed that the frontier myth has been "wrought into the very warp and woof of American thought."[13] Subsequent history has, if anything, confirmed his assessment of the American character; the end of the nineteenth century did not signal the demise of the frontier myth, only its relocation and reconceptualization. Consequently, the persistence of that myth raises important questions for us today: What is the relationship between national identity and geographical boundaries? Do contemporary political, military, and legislative attacks against "illegal aliens" suggest that the United States of today perceives national identity as still linked to the frontier, even if today we prefer the language of borders to that of frontiers?

THE BORDER AS PLACE OF ENCOUNTER

We might find an answer to those questions by asking the people "from the other side of the border." The "savages" on the other side—the southern side—might provide for us an alternative understanding of that border, one less beholden to the frontier myth, for the Latin American perception of the border is rooted in the distinctive history of Latin America itself.[14] While the modern drive for territorial expansion and domination is at the heart of both the Iberian and British colonization of the Americas, the processes of expansion developed quite differently in the North and South:

> The difference was that in the north it was possible and convenient to push back the native inhabitants rather than to conquer and subdue them. What northern colonialists wanted was land [rather than slave labor]. The original inhabitants were a hindrance. So, instead of subjugating the Indians, they set about to push them off their lands, and eventually to exterminate them. If the myth in the Spanish colonies was that the Indians were like children who needed someone to govern them, the myth in the English colonies was that the Indians were nonpeople; they didn't exist, their lands were a vacuum. In north Georgia, in the middle of Cherokee County, there is a monument to a white man who was, so the monument says, "the first man to settle in these parts." And this, in a county that is still called "Cherokee"! This contrast in the colonizing process led to a "border" mentality in Mexico and much of Latin America, and a "frontier" mentality in the United States. Because the Spanish colonizers were forced to live with the original inhabitants of the land, a *mestizo* population and culture developed. . . . In contrast, in the lands to the north, the process and the myth were of a constantly moving frontier, pushing back the native inhabitants of the land, interacting with them as little as possible. There was civilization this side of the frontier; and a void at the other side. The West was to be "won." The western line, the frontier, was seen as the growing edge;

but it was expected to produce growth by mere expansion rather than by interaction.[15]

In the North, then, "civilization" would expand by means of extermination; in the South, it would expand by means of domination. As horrific as the latter was in many cases, it nevertheless allowed for intermixing of races and cultures, even if often violently. In the North, the border moved in only one direction, outward; in the South, the border allowed for movement in both directions. In the North, any movement back across the border was thus perceived as "an incursion of the forces of evil and backwardness into the realm of light and progress."[16]

When perceived as a frontier, the border is in fact the meeting point of savagery and civilization. However, the savagery revealed is that of any "civilization" that strives to expand by means of extermination; the savages we encounter on the border are ourselves. And that is why we fear any movement back across the border toward the North—not, ultimately, because we hate "those savages," but because we hate ourselves and must deny the reality of our own history. The faces of those "savages" are the mirrors of this nation's soul; they are the "dangerous memory" that is never quite fully repressed.[17] "It is precisely in that willful innocence," warns Justo González, "that guilt lies." "The reason why this country has refused to hear the truth in its own history," he adds, "is that as long as it is innocent of such truth, it does not have to deal with the injustices that lie at the heart of its power and its social order."[18]

Yet a border can function and be understood differently. Even if too often denied in practice, an alternative understanding of the border is implicit in the *mestizo* history of Latin America:

A border is the place at which two realities, two worldviews, two cultures, meet and interact. . . . At the border growth takes place by encounter, by mutual enrichment. A true border, a true place of encounter, is by nature permeable. It is not like medieval armor, but rather like skin. Our skin does set a limit to where our body begins and where it ends. Our skin also sets certain limits to our give-and-take with our environment, keeping out certain germs, helping us to select that in our environment which we are ready to absorb. But if we ever close up our skin, we die.[19]

Borders are necessary means of affirming differences. However, when those differences are seen as life-giving rather than threatening, the border can become a place of genuine encounter and interaction. The border then becomes the seedbed of new life, the birthplace of a new human community.

GOD CHOOSES WHAT THE WORLD REJECTS

Such a new human community is precisely what the gospel demands from us, for the Christ of the Gospels is revealed, above all, on the border. Jesus comes from Nazareth, in Galilee, meets his end in Jerusalem and, finally, returns to Galilee, where he appears to the apostles after his resurrection (Mk 14:28; Mt 26:32; 28:7, 10, 16). In some sense, then, Galilee is at the very center of God's self-revelation in Jesus Christ. When we inquire into the character of Galilee, we discover that Galilee "was an outer region, far from the center of Judaism in Jerusalem of Judea and a crossroads of the great caravan routes of the world. It was a region of mixed peoples and languages."[20] Contiguous with non-Jewish territories and geographically distant from Jerusalem, Galilee was often viewed by first-century Jews as "a Jewish enclave in the midst of 'unfriendly' gentile seas."[21] "The area as a whole," writes Richard Horsley, "was a frontier between the great empires in their historical struggles."[22]

The history of Galilee as contested land and a political cross-roads resulted in the emergence of popular cultural and religious practices that reflected that multicultural history. Like so many borderlands, Galilee at the time of Jesus was an area of ethnic intermixing, an area of *mestizaje*. In the Gospels this borderland takes on theological significance as the place that defines the very character of the Christian revelation, for the good news is incarnated in the person of Jesus Christ. As Elizondo writes, "The overwhelming originality of Christianity is the basic belief of our faith that not only did the Son of God become a *human being*, but he became *Jesus of Nazareth*. . . . Jesus was not simply a Jew, he was a Galilean Jew; throughout his life he and his disciples were identified as Galileans."[23] Jesus Christ's racial-cultural distinctiveness as a Jewish man from a borderland region is not merely accidental to the Christian *kerygma*; it is at the very heart of our Christian faith.

In order to understand the good news, then, we must understand the theological value (or, rather, anti-value) of Galilee. As in so many human societies in history, the ruling elites in Jesus' world attached a moral and, indeed, theological value to the racial-cultural differences of the Galileans. "In Galilee," Elizondo observes, "the Jews were looked down upon and despised by the others as they were in the rest of the world. . . . Their own Jewish people despised them as inferior and impure. Because of their mixture with others, they were marginated by their own people." In short, the Galilean Jews could not be trusted because, living in the borderland, their contact with people from the other side of the border had made them impure and untrustworthy.

"Scripturally speaking," Elizondo writes, "Galilee does not appear important in the unfolding drama of salvation and, culturally speaking, at the time of Jesus, it was rejected and despised by the Judean Jews because of the racial mixture of the area and its distance from the temple in Jerusalem." Yet it is precisely here, on the border between religious purity and impurity, between civilization and savagery, that God chooses to be revealed. As Elizondo puts it:

> The apparent non-importance and rejection of Galilee are the very bases for its all-important role in the historic eruption of God's saving plan for humanity. The human scandal of God's way does not begin with the cross, but with the historico-cultural incarnation of [God's] Son in Galilee. . . . What the world rejects, God chooses as his very own.[24]

The religious elite in Jerusalem rejected the very possibility of the Galilean borderland as a locus of God's revelation: "Search and you will see that no prophet is to rise from Galilee" (Jn 7:52). Nevertheless, it is here in the very midst of racial-cultural impurity, among "savages" and "barbarians," among the "ignorant" and "superstitious," that God takes on human flesh.

Moreover, it is in the midst of those racial-cultural outcasts that the resurrected Christ, the now-glorified Witness to God's power and love, will be encountered: "he has risen from the dead, and behold, he is going before you to Galilee; there you will see him" (Mt 28:7). Just as the ministry and mission that define Jesus Christ as Son of God had begun in the villages and countryside of Galilee, so will that ministry and mission find their eschatological fulfillment in Galilee: "there you will see him." Jesus' ministry will end where it began; it is in Galilee that his disciples will see the resurrected Jesus. The chosen place of God's self-revelation is where Jews and Gentiles live side by side; the culture of the borderland is the privileged locus of God's self-revelation, the birthplace of the post-resurrection church. Precisely because the church knows no borders, it will be found first and foremost *on* the border, as a witness to the sinfulness of all our attempts to erect barriers that separate "us" from "them," the "civilized" from the "uncivilized," the "pure" from the "impure," the "mature Christian" from the "immature Christian." The border remains, not as a barrier that excludes, but rather as a place of revelation and transformation. In the encounter with the human other from beyond the border is made possible an encounter with the divine Other who transcends all borders.

SAVAGES AS EVANGELIZERS

Many centuries after Christ, on the border between Europe and America, between North and South, between Western civilization and "savagery," the *mestizo* church of the Americas was born in the encounter between *la Virgen morena* (the dark-skinned virgin), or Our Lady of Guadalupe, and a poor indigenous man, Juan Diego. The appearance of Our Lady of Guadalupe in December of 1531 signals a turning point, or axial point, in the history of Latin American *mestizaje*; at the very heart of Mexican history stands the figure of Our Lady of Guadalupe. Here, another resurrection took place, the resurrection of the Mexican people out of the ashes of conquest— once again, a resurrection on the border. Among those ashes the Virgin of Guadalupe and Juan Diego dare to proclaim the good news to a people who had been decimated by their Spanish Christian conquerors. In so doing, Guadalupe and Juan Diego reveal themselves as the true evangelizers of the Americas.

The popular devotion to Our Lady of Guadalupe is based on the *Nican Mopohua*, a text written in Náhuatl, the language of the indigenous Nahua people. The events recounted take place in 1531, not long after the Nahua defeat at the hands of the invading Spanish *conquistadores*, ten years after the conquest of Mexico City.[25]

Juan Diego is the first person we encounter in the story; he is described as a *macehual*, a "low class but dignified Indian."[26] Having left his home during the night, Juan Diego travels to Tlatelolco to attend Mass and receive catechetical instruction from the Spanish Christians. On the way, he comes to a hill called Tepeyac, which "was well known to the Mexican world as the site where the goddess virgin-mother of the gods [Tonantzín] was venerated."[27] There he hears birds singing, a sound so beautiful that he imagines he must be in paradise.

Entranced by the beautiful music, Juan Diego feels compelled to follow the sounds to their origins. As he seeks the source of the music, he hears a soft voice calling to him: "Quihuia; Iuantzin Iuan Diegotzin." These words have been translated into Spanish as "Juanito, Juan Dieguito" or "digno Juan, digno Juan Diego." The first translation, using the diminutive form of the name, suggests a special intimacy and affection; the speaker clearly feels a special love toward Juan Diego. The second translation emphasizes the speaker's recognition of Juan Diego's dignity as someone worthy of special respect. In Náhuatl, "*tzin* is a suffix which indicates respect, dignity and also familial affection."[28]

Juan Diego follows the sound of the voice and eventually comes to the top of the hill, where he sees a beautiful "Lady," radiantly dressed. She beckons him and, in an affectionate tone, asks: "Juanito, the dearest of my children, where are you going?" (63). Juan Diego tells the Lady that he is on his way to "her house in Mexico/Tlatelolco to hear about the divine things which are given and taught to us by our priests, the images [or delegates] of Our Lord." She then identifies herself as the Virgin Mary: "Know and rest assured in your heart, my dearest child, that I am the Ever Virgin Mary, Mother of the God of Great Truth, *Téotl*, of Him by Whom we live, of the Creator of Persons, of the Master [literally, Owner] of what is Close and Together, of the Lord of Heaven and Earth" (68). Thus, Mary identifies not only herself but also the Christian God *(Dios)* with the Nahua deity *Téotl*. She then orders Juan Diego to ask the bishop to build a temple on this hill so that from that place she could "show and give all her love, compassion, assistance, and protection to the people." Although Juan Diego had informed her that he was going to "her house" in Mexico (the seat of the bishop and center of the Spanish missionary efforts), she replies that, instead, her house should be built here, at Tepeyac (68–69). It is from here that she will evangelize her people.

When he arrives at the bishop's palace, Juan Diego is forced to wait a long time before being allowed to see the bishop, Juan de Zumárraga. After receiving Juan Diego, the bishop nevertheless asks him to return some other day, when he (the bishop) is less busy. Understandably disappointed, Juan Diego returns to Tepeyac to present his report to the Lady: "My Mistress, my Lady, the dearest of my Daughters, my Girl, I went where you sent me to tell your thoughts and words. Although with great difficulty I entered the place of the Lord of the priests, I saw him, and before him expressed your thoughts and words, just as you ordered. . . . But, I could tell by the way he responded that his heart did not accept it, he did not believe" (73).[29] Blaming himself for the failed mission, Juan Diego then asks the Lady to send someone else to the bishop, someone worthier, of greater stature: "Because, for sure, I am a meager peasant, a cord, a little ladder, the people's excrement, I am a leaf" (74). The Lady rejects his plea. Addressing him as "the dearest of my children," she insists that Juan Diego will be her chosen envoy and orders him to try again.

Obediently, Juan Diego returns to the bishop's palace the next day. This time the bishop asks Juan Diego many detailed questions about his story but, once again, turns Juan Diego away. The bishop requests from Juan Diego a sign that his story is true, that the Virgin has indeed appeared to him. Yet again, Juan Diego returns to Tepeyac to report on his visit with the bishop: "But even though he [the bishop] was told everything, how she looked, and everything he had seen and admired, through which she was rightly revealed as the beloved, ever Virgin, the wondrous Mother of Our Savior and Our Lord Jesus Christ, yet still he did not believe" (78).[30] The Lady responds by asking the indigenous man to return to

Tepeyac the next day, at which time she will give him an appropriate sign for the bishop.

When Juan Diego eventually returns to Tepeyac, the Lady asks him to go to the top of a nearby hill. There he will find wild flowers, which he should then cut and bring to her. Complying with her order, he is amazed to discover beautiful roses blooming on the hill, a natural impossibility in the middle of December. Honoring the Lady's wishes, he cuts the roses and brings them to her. The Lady then places the flowers in his *tilma*, or mantle, and orders him to take the roses to the bishop as the sign he had demanded. Surely the bishop would acknowledge that only a miracle could make such beautiful flowers bloom in December.

Once again, then, Juan Diego travels to the bishop's palace. Even though the Lady had ordered Juan Diego to open his mantle and show the flowers "only in the presence of the bishop" (86), the bishop's servants are intensely curious to see what the Indian man is carrying. They insist on seeing what he is carrying in his mantle and convince Juan Diego to give them a peek at the flowers. After entering to see the bishop this third time, Juan Diego unfolds his *tilma*, from which cascade to the floor the many beautiful roses he had picked. At that moment, the "beautiful image of the ever Virgin Mary, Mother of the God *Téotl*" suddenly appears on the *tilma*. Everyone present falls to their knees in wonder and homage. The bishop finally believes; he invites Juan Diego to stay overnight in the palace and orders the construction of the temple on Tepeyac. The image of the Lady is still visible today on Juan Diego's *tilma*, which is on display at the Shrine of Our Lady of Guadalupe, a magnificent modern version of the original church that today stands not far from the hill of Tepeyac.

The image itself is a powerful example of *mestizaje* in that it combines an array of Christian symbols with symbols indigenous to the Amerindian world of Juan Diego. One finds in the image, for example, numerous symbols of new life, a new beginning, and a new birth: the Lady is pictured as pregnant, she is wearing a "maternity band" around her waist, and she bears on her womb the symbol which, for the Nahuas, represented the "reconciliation of opposites."[31] The most obvious symbol, of course, is the color of the Lady's skin. To Western Christians accustomed to images of a blond and blue-eyed Mary, this Lady must surely appear incongruous; her olive skin tells the indigenous people of Mexico that she, *La Morenita*, is one of them. It tells all Mexicans and, indeed, all Latinos that she is one of them. This connection between the Lady and her children is powerfully symbolized by her eyes, in which are reflected the image of Juan Diego himself.[32]

The symbolism and narrative thus reflect the history of Mexico and Latin America as a *mestizo* people, a rich mixture of different races and cultures. In the figures of *La Morenita* and Juan Diego, God becomes identified with those peoples, cultures, and races who have been marginalized and rejected, the "savages" beyond the border. Guadalupe represents God's affirmation of the inherent dignity of those whom the European conquerors had deemed to be godless heathens. If Juan Diego is to be evangelized, it will be through a dark-skinned Lady on Tepeyac, the sacred place of the Nahuas, not through a Spanish bishop in his palace. Indeed, through Guadalupe, the very relationship between evangelizer and evangelized is reversed: the indigenous man, Juan Diego, is sent to evangelize the bishop. The traditional roles are thereby reversed. The dark-skinned Lady and the indigenous man themselves become the messengers of God, evangelizers to the Spanish Catholic bishop, who is portrayed as the one in need of conversion. The true missionary is not the bishop but Juan Diego. If the bishop had brought the God of conquest to the Americas, Juan Diego brings the God of the poor, the God of Galilee, to the Spanish bishop.

By revealing a Christian God with a special predilection for Juan Diego and his people, Guadalupe thus makes possible the evangelization of America. Without the hope engendered by *La Morenita* and her message, Mexico would not have emerged, like the phoenix, from the ashes of the conquest. This direct, historical connection between Guadalupe and Mexican identity is an important source of the passion with which her people celebrate and venerate *La Morenita*. In Guadalupe, the Mexican people have come to know the reality and power of Christ's resurrection, not as an abstract belief, but as a historical reality—a reality once again encountered in Galilee, on the border between civilization and savagery. And, once again, it's the "savages" beyond the border, beyond the frontier, who are revealed as children of God, the privileged bearers of the good news.

Our Lady of Guadalupe, Juan Diego, Pope John Paul II, and above all, the crucified and risen Galilean Jew thus challenge us today to reject the frontier myth that erects fences at the border, that views the border as the meeting point between savagery and civilization. They call us, instead, to go to the border, for "there we will see him"; there we will see the crucified and risen Christ and the dark-skinned Virgin. How we view the border and its inhabitants, then, is not merely a question of charity or justice (though it is that); it is, more profoundly still, a question of our own salvation, our own liberation. Let us not once again, then, like Bishop Juan de Zumárraga five centuries ago, turn away Juan Diego as he approaches us bearing in his *tilma* the precious gift of God's great love for *all* of us.

NOTES

[1] On this theme, see Jon Sobrino, *Spirituality of Liberation* (Maryknoll, NY: Orbis Books, 1988).

[2] Justo González, *Mañana* (Nashville, TN: Abingdon Press, 1990), 37.

[3] Alfred Lord Tennyson, *Ulysses,* as quoted in Frederick Jackson Turner, *Rereading Frederick Jackson Turner* (New York: Henry Holt and Co., 1994), 158.

[4] Ibid., 101. Latin American historian Enrique Dussel argues that, as the first European to extend European civilization westward, Christopher Columbus was the first "modern" person. Modernity is defined by the need to conquer and subdue: "Columbus thus initiated modernity. . . . Because of his departure from Latin anti-Muslim Europe, the idea that the Occident was the center of history was inaugurated and came to pervade the European life world. Europe even projected its presumed centrality upon its own origins. Hence, Europeans thought either that Adam and Eve were Europeans or that their story portrayed the original myth of Europe to the exclusion of other cultures" (Enrique Dussel, *The Invention of the Americas: Eclipse of "the Other" and the Myth of Modernity* [New York: Continuum, 1995], 32).

[5] Turner, *Rereading Frederick Jackson Turner*, 32, 60.

[6] John Mack Faragher, "Introduction," in ibid., 1.

[7] Turner, *Rereading Frederick Jackson Turner*, 96.

[8] Ray Allen Billington, *The Genesis of the Frontier Thesis: A Study in Historical Creativity* (San Marino, CA: The Huntington Library, 1971), 72.

[9] Walter LaFeber, *Inevitable Revolutions: The United States in Central America* (New York: W. W. Norton and Company, 1983), 300. Nevertheless, when the economic leverage weakened—for example, during the period between the Eisenhower and Reagan presidencies—economic expansion might require renewed political and military fortification.

[10] James G. Blaine, as quoted in ibid., 33.

[11] Ibid., 35.

[12] Ibid., 36, 39. The racist world view underlying these statements is only too clear, especially when one compares U.S. attitudes toward immigration from Mexico with the very different attitudes toward immigration from Europe—at least white, Anglo-Saxon, Protestant Europe.

[13] Turner, *Rereading Frederick Jackson Turner*, 96.

[14] Different notions of *border* are already embedded in the English and Spanish languages themselves. As Justo González notes, "Significantly, in English we say 'border,' and in Spanish, *frontera*. But when we translate the Spanish *frontera* back into English we can come up with either 'border' or 'frontier.' In fact, commonly used Spanish has no equivalent to the English 'frontier' as distinguished

from 'border'" (*Santa Biblia: The Bible through Hispanic Eyes* [Nashville, TN: Abingdon Press, 1996], 84).

[15] Ibid., 85–86.

[16] Ibid., 86. If one compares, for instance, the view of national borders represented by the North American Free Trade Agreement with that represented by California's Propositions 187 and 209, the 1996 Welfare Reform Act denying welfare benefits to documented immigrants and their children, and much more recent attempts to deny immigrants basic human rights, one receives a clear message: the United States will accord a freedom of movement to financial capital that it will not accord to mere human beings. The natural right of capital ("market forces," the "law" of supply and demand, "free" trade) to expand into new global markets must be affirmed as absolute and inviolable, while the right of labor (that is, human beings) to do so must be artificially restricted.

[17] Johann Baptist Metz, *Faith in History and Society: Toward a Practical Fundamental Theology* (New York: Seabury Press, 1980), 109.

[18] González, *Mañana*, 39.

[19] González, *Santa Biblia*, 86–87.

[20] Virgilio Elizondo, "Elements for a Mexican American Mestizo Christology," *Voices from the Third World* 11 (December 1988): 105.

[21] Douglas Edwards, "The Socio-Economic and Cultural Ethos of the Lower Galilee in the First Century: Implications for the Nascent Jesus Movement," in *The Galilee in Late Antiquity*, ed. Lee Levine (New York: Jewish Theological Seminary of America, 1992), 54.

[22] Richard A. Horsley, *Galilee: History, Politics, People* (Valley Forge, PA: Trinity Press International, 1995), 241.

[23] Virgilio Elizondo, *Galilean Journey: The Mexican-American Promise* (Maryknoll, NY: Orbis Books, 1983), 49.

[24] Elizondo, "Elements for a Mexican American Mestizo Christology," 105, 53.

[25] Clodomiro L. Siller Acuña, *Para comprender el mensaje de María de Guadalupe* (Buenos Aires: Editorial Guadalupe, 1989), 58. Siller provides the complete text of the story with a commentary. It is important to note that some scholars have raised serious questions about the origins of the Guadalupan narrative. For example, see Stafford Poole, *Our Lady of Guadalupe: The Origins and Sources*

of a Mexican National Symbol, 1531–1797 (Tucson: University of Arizona Press, 1995). Other scholars have, in turn, raised methodological questions about these revisionist critiques themselves. For instance, see Richard Nebel, *Santa María Tonantzín, Virgen de Guadalupe: Continuidad y transformación religiosa en México* (Mexico City: Fondo de Cultura Económica, 1995). A serious, systematic analysis of this debate is beyond the scope of this chapter. My concern here is to analyze the explicit content of the narrative itself. Thus, for example, I assume the narrative's identification of *La Morenita* with Mary (though, as mentioned above, with clear allusions to Tonantzín). A provocative, alternative interpretation is developed by Orlando Espín, who suggests that, in the light of popular practice, the Marian language might perhaps be better understood in pneumatological categories (*The Faith of the People: Theological Reflections on Popular Catholicism* [Maryknoll, NY: Orbis Books, 1997], 8–10).

[26] Virgilio Elizondo, *Guadalupe: Mother of the New Creation* (Maryknoll, NY: Orbis Books, 1997), 40.

[27] Virgilio Elizondo, *La Morenita: Evangelizer of the Americas* (San Antonio: Mexican American Cultural Center Press, 1980), 72.

[28] Siller, *Para comprender el mensaje de María de Guadalupe*, 63. Page numbers in the text refer to this book.

[29] See also Elizondo, *La Morenita*, 77.

[30] See also Jeanette Rodríguez, *Our Lady of Guadalupe: Faith and Empowerment among Mexican-American Women* (Austin: University of Texas Press, 1994), 42.

[31] Elizondo, *La Morenita*, 83; Rodríguez, *Our Lady of Guadalupe*, 22–30.

[32] Rodríguez, *Our Lady of Guadalupe*, 27.

12

Give Us the Joy of Hospitality

Samuel Wells

Boundless God,
in the infant Jesus you were a refugee
and among your own people you had no
    place to rest your head.

We pray for those who come to this land
    looking over their shoulder,
searching for safety, or protection, or the
    ability to support their households;
and we pray for those who find in this
    nation's people, ideals, and history
an inspiration for their own quest, their
    own vision, and their own hope.

Give us the discipline and joy of hospitality,
that we might see in the stranger both a
    reflection of our own pilgrim soul,
and an incarnation of your promise to be
    present in the least and the lost.

Help us to know when to open our homes,
    our hearts, our wallets, and our lives

to make room for the diverse and
    challenging ways you come among us.

And in all things make us ready to meet
    you,
when that moment comes when we are no
    longer at home
but stand at your door, begging to be your
    guest.

Through Jesus Christ our Lord.
Amen.

13

Resisting Eco-Injustice, Watering the Garden

Larry L. Rasmussen

"Why do the injuries of nature delight you?" Saint Ambrose asked in fourth-century Milan, a bustling center of the Roman Empire.

> The world has been created for all, while you rich are trying to keep it for yourselves. Not merely the possession of the earth, but the very sky, air and the sea are claimed for the use of the rich few. . . . Not from your own do you bestow on the poor man, but you make return from what is his. For what has been given as common for the use of all, you appropriate for yourself alone. The earth belongs to all, not to the rich.[1]

Sections of this chapter draw upon the author's following works: "Environmental Apartheid," in *Earth Community, Earth Ethics* (Maryknoll, NY: Orbis Books, 1996), 75–89; "Environmental Racism and Environmental Justice: Moral Theory in the Making?" in *Journal of the Society of Christian Ethics* 24, no. 1 (2004): 3–28; and "Drilling in the Cathedral," in *Dialog: A Journal of Theology* (Fall 2003): 202–225.

The heart of Christian prophetic-liberative traditions is justice-centered faith. Its key is shared and saving power for the healing and thriving of creation. Ambrose assumes that so long as rich oppress poor and a good in common is not achieved, so long will "the injuries of nature delight" some.

A widely quoted eighteenth-century quatrain protesting the English Enclosure Act might also have introduced this chapter on resisting eco-injustice:

> The law doth punish man or woman
> That steals the goose from the common,
> But lets the greater felon loose,
> That steals the commons from the goose.

Neither theft is commended. But to steal earth as "our one and all, the first condition of our existence" is the greater felony.[2] Attaching lot to lot (Isaiah), selling the poor for a pair of shoes (Amos), and possessing for exploitation not only "the earth, but the very sky, air and the sea" (Ambrose) is robbery of the kind that cries out to heaven.

Still, the prophetic railing and renunciations of Isaiah, Amos, Hosea, Joel, and Jeremiah are the rage side of a violated vision and a dream deferred. Their language is confrontational, full of warning and judgment. Their call is to repent, to turn from a destructive way of life and toward the beloved community and a peaceable kingdom. Thus railing and rage are not the baselines or the fuels that burn with prophetic energy. Hope and redemption, peace and abundance, creation redeemed are. A beautiful world in God, beautiful even "beyond the singing of it," is the burden the prophets bear.[3] Kept covenants and songs of new creation lift their voice. Hope is always hope for creation as a whole, land and people together. Liberation is the liberation of all life, a struggle that necessarily includes the poor, the weak, the diseased, and disfigured. And not least, exploited and exhausted nature is renewed. Salvation is good health everywhere and for all.

This is where the Bible begins, at least chronologically: with the account of redemption as freedom secured for slaves. The God of mercy and compassion, who creates a people from those who were none and hues a way where there was none, "knows" (experiences) the suffering of those who toil under Pharaoh and goes before in the long and harsh journey to a teeming land and fertile Sabbath.

Here, in Hebrew scripture's very beginning, and later in the prophet's driving dreams, is the picture of life abundant and harmonious, with all nations streaming to Zion's mountain, itself rising from the redeemed plain, as celebrated in Jeremiah 31:12–14:

> They shall come and sing aloud on the
>   height of Zion,
> and they shall be radiant over the goodness
>   of the Lord,
> over the grain, the wine, and the oil,
> and over the young of the flock and the herd;
> their life shall become like a watered
>   garden, and they shall never languish
>   again.
> Then shall the young women rejoice in the
>   dance,
> and the young men and the old shall be
>   merry.
> I will turn their mourning into joy,
> I will comfort them, and give them gladness
>   for sorrow.
> I will give the priests their fill of fatness,
> and my people shall be satisfied with my
>   bounty, says the Lord.

In this tradition the life of faith issues in justice-centered living. Righteousness is the core theme, right relations with all that is—one another, the land, the rest of nature, and the

God whose first and everlasting covenant is with Earth itself and "every living creature of all flesh" (Gn 9). The fullest possible flourishing of all life is the very definition of justice in this account. When justice is done, *shalom* and abundance follow. But until it is done, the vineyards languish, the merry-hearted sigh, and the earth is polluted and cursed (Is 24:5–7).

The prophets, then, are utterly clear: when the people of God are just in their relations in and to the community—themselves, the animals, the land, together—their sacrifices are pleasing to the Lord. When they act without restraint and amass agricultural surplus and wealth at the expense of workers and the land, their sacrifices stink to high heaven. The injuries of nature may continue to delight them, but they offend the Lord God Jehovah, who will not listen to the noise "of [their] solemn assemblies" (Am 5:21).

Despite these biblical roots, it took James Cone to point out what Martin Luther King Jr., immersed in this biblical stream, kept insisting—that justice is an essential, not secondary, ingredient of Christianity, although few Christian theologians have made it their starting point or ending point.

THE ENVIRONMENTAL JUSTICE MOVEMENT

The environmental justice movement is at home here, in the prophetic-liberative tradition. While its official launch was the First National People of Color Environmental Leadership Summit in Washington DC in 1991, its roots are sunk much deeper, deep in the experience of those who suffered the fact that the United States was a settler nation and a slave-holding one in the formative centuries of its existence. Life has always been toxic on the "wrong side" of the tracks, and resistance of one kind or another has always been present, from noncooperation to armed rebellion to underground railways to mass nonviolent protest to the baleful sounds of the spirituals and the blues.

It was not, then, the modern environmentalist movement of preservation and conservation of wild places that generated the environmental justice movement. It was not the work or spinoff of the "big ten"—The Sierra Club, World Wildlife Fund, the Natural Resources Defense Council, and others. On the contrary, their neglect of the rural and urban poor of marginal standing, together with crowded urban neighborhoods and degraded rural lands, sparked the environmental justice movement. People whose genes and long memories know reservation lands, slave quarters, a trail of broken treaties, forced residence and forced working of the land, together with forced removal of it, endemic bad health, vulnerability to the ravages of nature, and too few resources to survive well, gave birth to the environmental justice movement. Racism, classism, and a narrow construal of environmentalism—these echoes of Ambrose called the movement into being.

Differently said, the deep memory of the environmental justice movement trails back to the first wave of economic globalization. If a single symbol were chosen, it might be the great cathedral of Seville, Spain. In one poorly lighted segment of this vast space, the sepulcher of Christopher Columbus is carried by four men in regal apparel, the figures and the casket alike astride an imposing pedestal. A short distance away the Chapel of the Antiguas flies an array of flags, the flags of imperial Spain and the Americas. A bronze plaque explains the decor: "the first voyage around the globe began and ended in this chapel." Columbus and his sailor successors had learned to cross the two great oceans, the Atlantic and Pacific. That initiated the Age of Discovery, which, in turn, established neo-European societies on every single continent except Antarctica.

Isabella and Ferdinand, the Catholic monarchs celebrated by this great cathedral, had, also in 1492, banished Muslims and Jews from Spain (or offered them conversion to Christianity as the alternative) and laid claim to the world in the name of Roman Christianity and the newly "cleansed" and unified Spain. A pope friendly to their mission, Pope Alexander VI, cooperated generously with the "Bull of Donation." It simply gave—donated—all islands and main lands "discovered and to be discovered, one hundred leagues to the West and South from . . . the Azores and Cape Verde," and not already occupied or held by any Christian king or prince as of Christmas 1492, to Isabella and Ferdinand.[4] The pope was clear: European Christian monarchs should rule the world, spread civilization, and save the benighted souls of non-Christian brothers and sisters with the choice of baptism, the sword, or both.

Together with the expeditions and exploits of other Christian monarchs, this marked the beginning of the movement of political-economic globalization in its first and most decisive phase. The planet was to be encircled in a web of conquest and colonization, commerce and Christianity, bundled together as civilization and the subordination of all lands and peoples to white Christian rule. The Middle Passage had begun, as had the devastation of native peoples of the Americas by guns, germs, and steel. The "civilizing mission" of "superior" peoples and cultures over "inferior" ones was under way. And, most important for our concern, consequences flowing from the patterns of privilege and power accomplished in that initial wave of globalization last to this day.

Superiority of such a racist and cultural cast was brutal. Native peoples were killed, moved out, or assimilated, all on neo-European terms; even more died from the European-borne diseases for which they had no immunity. African slaves who survived the Middle Passage faced centuries of ensuing threat and fear, while native peoples were forced to make do with a miniscule portion of their previous homelands (and often the least resource-rich and desirable portion).

The underlying morality of Christian conquest, colonization, and commerce was both chilling and theological. "Again and again during the centuries of European imperialism," writes environmental historian Alfred Crosby, "the Christian view that all men are brothers was to lead to persecution of non-Europeans—he who is my brother sins to the extent that he is unlike me."[5] White and European was the marker and norm, and living as brothers and sisters required conforming to this norm. Furthermore, land and waters, too, were forced to cede their profound sense of place to colonial and imperial ways, whether those ways were appropriate to the innate powers of the bioregions and continents or not. A domination ethic prevailed from sea to shining sea, and for all domains between.

Even later development of more democratic polities failed to wrest the play of power and privilege from this pattern of white supremacy and its androcentric, neo-European treatment of nature. As late as 1957, William F. Buckley Jr., guru of conservative Republican thought and editor of the highly influential *National Review,* responded to the famous U.S. Supreme Court decision on *Brown v. Board of Education* in this way:

> The central question that emerges—and it is not a parliamentary question or a question that is answered by merely consulting a catalogue of rights of American citizens, born equal—is whether the White community in the South is entitled to take such measures as are necessary to prevail, politically and culturally, in areas where it does not predominate numerically? The answer is Yes—the White community is so entitled because, for the time being, it is the advanced race. . . . *National Review* believes that the South's premises are correct. If the majority wills what is socially atavistic, then to thwart the majority may be, though undemocratic, enlightened. . . . Universal suffrage is not the beginning of wisdom or the beginning of freedom.[6]

Such is the legacy shaping the environmental justice movement—on the one hand, the prophetic-liberative traditions of moral and religious substance and feeling, and on the other, peoples and lands who have suffered the long reign of an imperial and instrumental logic that "defines everything and everybody in terms of their contribution to the development and defense of white world supremacy."[7] Any account of environmentalism that discusses human alienation from nature and the land without this history of white supremacy is an intellectual crime as well as a theological and moral one. The equality of children of God, all of whom bear the same image and share the same status, is denied where it counts—in life together and in practice. Cone's double formulation remains dead-on correct: "People who fight against white racism but fail to connect it to the degradation of the earth are anti-ecological—whether they know it or not. People who struggle against environmental degradation but do not incorporate it in a disciplined and sustained fight against white supremacy are racists—whether they acknowledge it or not. The fight for justice cannot be segregated but must be integrated with the fight for life in all its forms."[8]

I write this on January 15, the anniversary of Martin Luther King Jr.'s birth. King and the civil rights movement belong to environmental justice memory and consciousness as well. One canonical memory is King's last campaign, cut short by his assassination. It was on behalf of striking garbage workers in Memphis, workers carrying placards asking for a fair wage, recognition, and dignity. "I am a Man," they read. Civil rights struggles bridged over to environmental justice ones. This kind of memory also gave rise to the term *environmental racism*. It was the charge shouted by a young woman at a 1982 protest in Warren County, North Carolina, against more trash dumped in poor communities, this time in the form of a PCB landfill in that predominantly African American county. "This here is nothin' but *environmental racism*," she said.[9] With that, the experience of generations rose to the surface and the term stuck.

The term soon found its public voice and ample evidence in the United Church of Christ's landmark study *Toxic Wastes and Race in the United States*. The authors were not Environmental Protection Agency (EPA) employees or members of the business community but the staff of the small office of the United Church of Christ Commission for Racial Justice at the Interchurch Center in New York City.[10] Using U.S. census data and government data on the location of hazardous-waste sites, the report documented environmental racism and helped spark the environmental justice movement. Later studies, including those of the EPA, confirmed what *Toxic Wastes and Race in the United States* showed: three in five African Americans lived in communities with abandoned toxic-waste sites. Three of the five largest commercial hazardous-waste landfills were in predominantly African American or Latino American communities. These accounted for approximately 40 percent of the nation's estimated landfill capacity. Overall, poorer communities fared far worse than affluent ones as sites of commercial toxic waste, and poorer people of color fared worse than poor whites. Since poor women and children, especially poor women and children of color, fared worse than men in most communities, negative gender and generational factors correlated as well.

In a word, race, class, age, and gender were all intersected by systemically biased environmental practices. Different communities suffered different consequences. They didn't all breathe the same air, drink the same water, or sail in the same boat. Injustice was authorized, authorized by privilege and the way privilege organized power and practice.

In 2007 the United Church of Christ revisited these earlier findings and issued *Toxic Wastes and Race at Twenty, 1987–2007*. This new report documents the real victories that followed the national and worldwide attention the original study evoked, together with the resistance to being dumped on that it spawned in countless locales. Yet the racial and socioeconomic disparities have persisted, and the conclusions in the 2007 report parallel those of 1987—namely, race matters, place matters, class and gender matter. Unequal protection still places communities of color at special risk; the most polluting industries still go to the places where land, labor, and lives are cheap as they chase profits and the bottom line around the globe; and current environmental protection still fails to provide equal protection to low-income communities of people of color. In part these patterns persist because the mission of the EPA was never to address unfair, unjust, and inequitable outcomes of environmental policies and practices. President Clinton did mandate environmental impact studies for federal government policies—one of those victories of the resistance spawned by *Toxic Wastes and Race in the United States* and environmental justice action—but that was done precisely because it was not included in the EPA mission.

The twenty-year report devotes three pages to concrete recommendations for congressional and executive branches and state and local governments, together with nongovernmental community organizations.

Not long after the 1987 report, and stimulated in part by it, the First National People of Color Environmental Leadership Summit was convened in Washington DC (October 1991). It adopted seventeen principles of environmental justice, the first of which reads: "Environmental justice affirms the sacredness of Mother Earth, ecological unity and the interdependence of all species, and the right to be free from ecological destruction." Yet it is the preamble that makes clear the provenance of this and the remaining principles:

> We, the people of color, gathered together at this multinational People of Color Environmental Leadership Summit, to begin to build a national and international movement of all peoples of color to fight the destruction and taking of our lands and communities, do hereby reestablish our spiritual interdependence to the sacredness of our Mother Earth; to respect and celebrate each of our cultures, languages and beliefs about the natural world and our roles in healing ourselves; to insure

environmental justice; to promote economic alternatives which would contribute to the development of environmentally safe livelihoods; and, to secure our political, economic and cultural liberation that has been denied for over 500 years of colonization and oppression, resulting in the poisoning of our communities and land and the genocide of our peoples, do affirm and adopt these Principles of Environmental Justice.[11]

The second summit, a decade later in September 2002, was planned for five hundred representatives. Fourteen hundred arrived.

Yet waste is not the half of it, as the environmental justice movement knows full well. It is only one item among the consequences that flow from current global industry, trade, and finance. The truly generative factors of eco-injustice are historically unprecedented extraction of renewable and nonrenewable resources; the processing, distribution, and consumption of these for global markets (waste is a spinoff of this); and the competitive scramble to find cheaper resources and take advantage of low wages and less stringent environmental conditions. When these factors interact as the deadly dance of the global political economy, they generate cumulative social and environmental consequences for the people and the rest of nature in a given locale. The cumulative impact often includes the fraying of community bonds, with psychic and cultural consequences, as well as the depleting of community resources.

A recent front-page account in *The New York Times* vividly illustrates all of this. "Europe Takes Africa's Fish, and Migrants Follow" is the first in a series on "empty seas." The report opens with the story of Ale Nodye, a Senegalese fisherman who is the son and grandson of fishermen. He had captained a canoe filled with eighty-seven Africans who headed for the Canary Islands in hopes of finding their way from there to Europe. All were arrested and deported. But Ale says he must try again, since "there are no fish in the sea here anymore." "Many scientists agree," the account continues. The reason is that "a large flotilla of industrial trawlers from the European Union, China, Russia and elsewhere, together with an abundance of local boats, have so thoroughly scoured northwest Africa's ocean floor that major fish populations are collapsing." Consequently, coastal communities and traditional ways of life are collapsing as well, and to date roughly thirty-one thousand Africans have tried to reach the Canary Islands en route to Europe in search of work. The Europeans themselves have largely fished out their own waters and so have steered their subsidized fleets to Africa. They have found strapped African governments, some of them corrupt, that are willing to sell fishing rights to them, even against the interest of their own coastal communities. Back in Europe, more stringent environmental laws work to restore the depleted fisheries. Thus the European (and Chinese) boats go south to maintain their own livelihoods at the same time that citizens of the north resist the tide of environmental refugees from Africa.[12]

The pattern is the old, familiar one in place since the Age of Discovery and its imperial reach: extraction and displacement. But it is intensified now by far greater consumption in affluent strata worldwide and far more people.

The outcome is equally familiar, articulated a long while ago by Frederick Engels:

> To make earth an object of huckstering—the earth which is our one and all, the first condition of our existence— was the last step towards making oneself an object of huckstering. It was and is to this day an immorality surpassed only by the immorality of self-alienation. And the original appropriation—the monopolization of the earth by a few, the exclusion of the rest from that which is the condition of their life—yields nothing in immorality to the subsequent huckstering of the earth.[13]

That line ("the original appropriation—the monopolization of the earth by a few, the exclusion of the rest from that which is the condition of their life—yields nothing in immorality to the subsequent huckstering of the earth") is almost a paraphrase of the quotation from Saint Ambrose at this chapter's onset. Not surprisingly, the final conclusion must thus be the same as well: short of radical social transformation, eco-injustice will persist. So will, we trust, prophetic-liberative resistance. Yet now that "the injuries of nature" and "the huckstering of the earth" have gone global with a vengeance, the need for Christian resistance in the twenty-first century will be greater, not lesser. Until that day, to play on the words of early twentieth-century poet and writer Clifford Bax, "earth will not be fair, nor her peoples one."

NOTES

[1] St. Ambrose of Milan, *De Nabuthe Jezraelita* 3, 11.

[2] Frederick Engels, "Outlines of a Critique of Political Economy," in Karl Marx, *Economic and Philosophic Manuscripts of 1844* (Moscow: Foreign Languages Publishing House, 1856), 190.

[3] A phrase from the opening of Alan Paton's *Cry, the Beloved Country* (New York: Scribner's, 1948), 3. He writes of South Africa in the 1940s, the beloved but deeply flawed country, and here of the "lovely road that runs from Ixopo into the hills . . . lovely beyond any singing of it." The beauty of South Africa only made more wrenching and unacceptable the ugliness of its apartheid system.

[4] Alexander VI, "Inter Caetera," available online.

[5] Alfred W. Crosby, *The Columbian Exchange* (Westport, CT: Greenwood Press, 1974), 12.

[6] William F. Buckley Jr., "Why the South Must Prevail," *National Review* (August 24, 1957), 149.

[7] James H. Cone, "Whose Earth Is It, Anyway?" in *Habitat Earth: Eco-Injustice and the Church's Response*, ed. Dieter Hessel and Larry Rasmussen (Minneapolis, MN: Fortress Press, 2001), 23.

[8] Ibid.

[9] The United Church of Christ Commission for Racial Justice was an active organizer of the 1982 protest of five hundred or so people in Warren County after the State of North Carolina decided to locate a toxic waste landfill of PCBs in a community of primarily poor African Americans.

[10] Commission for Racial Justice, *Toxic Wastes and Race in the United States* (New York: United Church of Christ, 1987).

[11] "Principles of Environmental Justice," adopted at the First National People of Color Environmental Leadership Summit on October 27, 1991, Washington DC.

[12] "Europe Takes Africa's Fish, and Migrants Follow," *The New York Times*, January 14, 2008.

[13] Frederick Engels, "Outlines of a Critique of Political Economy," 190.

Help Us Love the World

Valerie Weaver-Zercher

Holy God of the Cosmos,
   Of distant stars and diving comets,
   Of spinning planets and radiant moons,
   Of wildness and immensity beyond our
      imagining—
Give us eyes to see.

Holy God of the Small Things,
   Who told stories about sparrows and
      lilies,
   Mustard seeds and kernels of grain,
   Who fashioned lizards and thrushes,
      violets and minnows—
Show us how to see the world.

(Silence)

Loving God of Humanity,
   Who wept when Lazarus died and
      turned over tables in fury,

Who resisted powerfully and loved
    extravagantly enough to die,
And who still longs to gather your
    children under your wings,
Give us hearts to love.

Loving God of All Things,
    You are hearing the groans of your
        creation.
    We have forgotten that all these good
        gifts belong to you.
    We have damaged and polluted your
        handiwork,
    and disregarded your call to be stewards.
    We have bruised the reed, and quenched
        the dimly burning wick.
Forgive us. Show us how to love the world.

(Silence)

Caring God,
    Who brings springs out of dry ground,
        and hope out of despair,
    Who turns penitence into creativity, and
        fear into faith,
    Show us how to repair the world.
Give us hands to care.

Caring God,
    Who spread out the earth on the waters
    And asked us to tend the garden:
    Give us now the tools we need for
        healing, and the soil for nurturing.
    Send us the rainfall of renewal, and the
        sunlight of hope.

Give us the talent for tending, and the
      persistence to labor.
Show us how to care for the world.

(Silence)

In seeing, may we learn to love.
In loving, may we learn to care.

O God, make us quiet and attentive enough
      to see creation,
   disciplined and joyful enough to cherish it,
   and zealous and hopeful enough to tend it.

O God of all sight, all love, and all caring,
Give us eyes to see, hearts to love, and
      hands to care for your world.

Amen.

Resisting Individualism, Advocating Solidarity

Douglas Sturm

AN AUTOBIOGRAPHICAL IRONY

Herbert Hoover was inaugurated president of the United States in 1929, the year of my birth. During his campaign for that office in 1928, he delivered a famed speech honoring "the American system of rugged individualism."[1]

Hoover's declaration was more than a campaign slogan. It was a settled conviction, evidenced in a brief text he authored in 1922 in which he declared, "Individualism has been the primary focus of American civilization for three centuries."[2]

Hoover distinguished "authentic American individualism" from its crude "dog eat dog" version. Both favor a principle of self-reliance, but the former is characterized by its promotion of equality of opportunity as a means of encouraging personal creativity and therefore human progress.

My father and mother, raised in rural families thoroughly imbued with that widespread American sensibility, were fervent supporters of Herbert Hoover. They took the individualist dream seriously when together they started their climb up the ladder of success. But then, in the months following my birth, the Great Depression turned that dream into a terrifying nightmare. The ladder of success had lost its rungs. Our family life tumbled into a time of turmoil and uncertainty.

Over the next twelve years we moved on average once a year. My father shifted from job to job—bank teller, insurance agent, factory worker, farmhand, gas-station manager—grasping at any way to provide basic support for his family. In the spring of 1941, at age thirty-nine, he died. The stress had overwhelmed him. The Great Depression had taken its toll. My mother became a single parent with two young sons. Once again, we moved—into a tiny three-room apartment. From that time we were without automobile and telephone. As a family, we had slipped completely off the ladder of success.

By this time, months before the United States officially entered World War II, Franklin Delano Roosevelt was beginning his third term as president of the United States. As the successor to Herbert Hoover, he was elected initially in response to the devastation wreaked by the Great Depression. The New Deal was constructed as a means of recovering prospects for a decent life among the American people, as a way, in a sense, of restoring the American dream.

Nonetheless, my father, as I learned during my childhood years, despised FDR and his New Deal. With others, he dubbed the New Deal's WPA project for unemployed men and women "We Putter Around." I still have among my family memorabilia a "No Third Term" button. To be fair, my father was, in my experience, a warmhearted, generous man, always prepared to assist those in need. Our home, even as we moved from site to site, was among those marked by hoboes and tramps as a welcoming place for a meal. Though my father was given to such acts of kindness, he remained, in his heart, a rugged individualist, determined to create, on his own, a decent life for himself and his family. He did his best. Yet at the time of his death, he was unemployed; his family was quartered temporarily in the homestead of his father-in-law, an elderly farmer; and he had no assets to pass on to his survivors.

Within a very brief time following my father's death, my mother and her two sons began receiving monthly checks, Survivor Benefits, from the Social Security Administration. That's the irony of this story. The New Deal, which my father had berated so adamantly, provided, as a matter of public policy, a modest but necessary supplement to the low wages my mother earned as a filing clerk in a nonunion factory. These monthly checks were a godsend. Even at my tender age, I was impressed. Yet I was insufficiently versed in the deeper dimensions of this irony to understand what was at stake in this turn of events. Very gradually it dawned on me.

Beginning about that time and continuing throughout my adolescence during the forties, I became increasingly exposed to many of the critical issues of the times. Their seriousness and implications contributed to a profound transformation of my comprehension of the world as well as my self-identity. Included among these issues were the agony of war, the systematic extermination of European Jews by the Nazis, the lynching of African Americans and their legalized segregation, poverty in the United States and abroad, and discrimination against ethnic minorities (including the oppression of indigenous peoples).

My introduction to these issues derived in part from the public schools and personal experience but also through active participation in the Methodist Youth Fellowship movement. Through the MYF, I began to discern, if only in an elementary way, that insights derived from the Hebrew prophets and the Synoptic Gospels provide a powerful way of interpreting and reacting to social issues. Influenced by this tradition, I became increasingly troubled with these issues as matters of injustice.

As my education about the state of the world proceeded, I began to see that American history since its beginnings has been, and remains, awash with serious contention over what life is all about and what vision should govern our common life.

The struggle between Hoover's rugged individualism and FDR's New Deal was among those differences, one that was prominent in the United States during the second quarter of the twentieth century and that continues to reverberate throughout the nation even yet. Efforts to tell the American story as if it were a linear unfolding of a single ideal gloss over these and other struggles that are manifest in every stage of the nation's history and that characterize debates in the public forum.

From this developing perspective I perceived that these contentious issues—at least the more far-reaching ones—are both religious and political. I am using these two words in a special (but not idiosyncratic) way. In *religious* I include all efforts to answer these questions: What is life all about? however traditional or nontraditional those efforts might be. By *political*, I mean all affirmations related to the question, What vision should govern our life together? These are two questions that, consciously or unconsciously, each and every one of us confronts. Even if we do not reflect about them extensively and even if we do not address them in traditional ways, our actions betray some kind of answer to them. While differing in focus, these two questions are not unrelated.

In what follows I invite readers to concentrate on two kinds of answers to this pair of questions. Both answers are among those currently at stake in struggles over the future of the world. They are contrasting world views—ways of comprehending our place in the world and how we should direct our lives and organize our interactions. For ease of reference, I shall designate them as contrasting principles: individualism and solidarity.

The former, the principle of individualism, bears an insight worthy of our commitment, but an insight that, over time, has been twisted to justify its perversion. The latter, the principle of solidarity, whose historical beginnings in the West include the covenantal tradition of Judaism and Christianity, is a far more adequate response to the massive challenges we now confront in our common life. We are called, I declare, to resist modern individualism, given its distortions and its basic flaw, and to bend our energies toward the advocacy of solidarity as a version of covenantalism.

WORDS AND WORLD VIEWS IN THE PUBLIC FORUM: A BRIEF EXCURSUS

Recently respected linguistics scholar George Lakoff published a series of essays about the use of words in the public forum.[3] His primary message is that words matter in ways we too often ignore. On the surface, words are intended to communicate thoughts and ideas, feelings and judgments, propositions and demands pertinent to the immediate circumstance. That's how we use them in everyday conversation.

In that process, of course, while words may usually be sincere and straightforward, they may also be used to tease, provoke, entertain, deceive, confuse, or manipulate the behavior of others. In all cases, however, words, if carefully apprehended and analyzed, express a deeper, more encompassing meaning.

Within the forum where public policies are under debate, then, we should recognize that often more is at stake than just the immediate policies themselves. At issue are differing visions of the political future, models for the shaping of our associations with each other. These visions constitute the long-range political intention of those engaged in the debate; that is, words employed within the context of the public forum, though directed immediately toward the formulation of specific policies, are efforts to create, more or less, a new political world or to perpetuate an old one.

Intriguingly, a similar understanding of the creative intent and potential power of words is evident in ancient religious stories. So, for instance, the story about beginnings in the opening passages of the Book of Genesis reports that God declared "let there be light" and that light came into being. As the story proceeds, God's speaking created an entire world that he pronounced "very good."

Might I suggest that, through that sacred story, its writers were affirming not only God's creativity but also the powerful creativity of humankind? The story, after all, insists that we are made in the image of the Divine. At the very least this suggests that we, too, possess the capacity to bring about new worlds. The future is, to some degree, contingent on how we think and communicate and act—though, of course, we must reflect critically on whether the worlds we would create are or are not "very good."

By public forum in this context I mean to include all those kinds of intercommunication, informal and formal, through which we as a people come to a mind about the issues that bother us and determine how to reconstruct the world, social and natural, that we inhabit. The public forum in this sense is a critical location through which historical change comes about. As such, the public forum embraces multiple circles of conversation; it is not limited to governmental institutions. Indeed, governmental institutions themselves are subjected now and then to revolutionary transformation because of the pressures of the surrounding public forum.

At first blush, conversations in the public forum focus on matters of policy over very particular issues, some more important than others. However, we acknowledge that those conversations and debates over policy convey deeper meanings when we distinguish among parties according to their "real interests," their constituencies, their ideologies or philosophies, and their long-range concerns.

Nowadays in the United States, we are quick to label parties liberal, conservative, leftwing, rightwing, libertarian, progressive, or radical. In the current language of political analysis, each party is prone to put its own spin on policy proposals represented in the language it employs.

So a forested mountain may be depicted as a rich economic resource or an ecological habitat. A new set of regulations for the work place may be dubbed an inefficient and costly bureaucratic interference or a constraint to protect the health and safety of workers. An obstetric procedure may be called partial birth abortion or intact D&X. The appropriation of land for public purposes may be deemed eminent domain invoked to serve the general welfare or the unfair confiscation of private property. A military action may be labeled a matter of national security or a humanitarian intervention.

Terms such as *conservatism* and *progressivism* are drawn upon to indicate positions along a spectrum of diverse political orientations, at each point on which we have learned to expect a characteristic way of talking about and responding to the matter under debate. Even when parties negotiate their differences, that process does not detract from their divergent mind sets.

These political orientations, I propose, reflect an even more fundamental dimension of meaning as they play out in public discourse, joining the two questions I have specified above: What vision should govern our life together? (the political question), and What is life all about? (the religious question). That is, debates in the public forum, particularly where the differences are sharp and may at moments prove to be irreconcilable, are reflective of divergent world views. We sometimes convey this divergence in the language of values and preference. However, it is more than that. In this dimension the divergence is over variant ways of comprehending the kind of world we inhabit at the present and the kind of world we intend to create in the future. It is over contrasting ways of understanding who we are, what our relationship is to our surroundings, and what we are determined to do to shape our tomorrows.

Within our expanding human community there are many such world views, some more prominent than others. Some are longstanding, considered traditions, passed on from generation to generation. Some are explicitly religious, and others fulfill a similar function even if considered secular. All of them over the course of time shift and change, merge and separate, even while retaining the same label.

Now to the point of this brief excursus: principles of individualism and solidarity are cases of world views currently at battle in the modern West. I concentrate on these two world views because of their prominence, but more specifically because, in my judgment, while individualism embodies a vital truth about our human identity, it is in the final analysis—particularly given its historical twists and turns—a basically inadequate response to the most critical challenges of our times. Its inadequacy is rooted in a flawed understanding of who we are and what our moral vocation is in the context of our surroundings. On that score, the principle of solidarity as a contemporary version of covenantalism, at least as I shall represent it, is a far more appropriate way to discern the moral crises we now confront and to direct our energies toward a just and sustainable future.

INDIVIDUALISM: ITS GENIUS AND ITS INVERSION

The emergence of individualism as a way of life in the West signified the remarkable transition from the medieval world to the modern world.[4] At its peak the medieval world was dominated by a vision of Christendom as an encompassing social system governed ultimately by an objective moral order. That moral order was the preserve of the Roman Catholic Church, acting through rulers, sacred and temporal, who were authorized to maintain appropriate laws and customs throughout the region. Individual persons in this conception occupy distinct roles within the system, identified by their assigned status and expected to act in accordance with their position in the hierarchical structure. To act out of synch with that structure was to incur punishment by church and state. That was the ideal, not always and everywhere fully realized, but it tended to prevail as an institutionalized normative standard throughout the thought and practice of medieval Europe. It was strictly hierarchical in structure, supernatural in aim, organic in texture.

The dramatic shift toward the modern Western world was a construction of multiple cultural forces over several centuries, including the Renaissance, with its humanistic focus derived from its appropriation of the Classical arts, and the Protestant Reformation, with its themes of justification by faith and the priesthood of all believers.

But perhaps the Enlightenment of the eighteenth century best encapsulated the spirit of modernity with its explicit turn toward the individual human subject. In a classic statement about the central meaning of this movement, philosopher Immanuel Kant declared the motto of the Enlightenment: "Have courage to use your own reason!"[5] In one simple phrase, that motto reveals the crux of individualism as a world view, setting it in sharp contrast to the medieval ideal of Christendom. We are instructed not to kowtow to tradition, not to give unquestioning obedience to presumed authorities, but to think and to act, each one of us, for ourselves. The adoption of that motto energized the development of new forms of science and philosophy, politics and economics, culture and religion, all of them manifesting, at least in their beginnings, implications of an individualistic world view.

Intriguingly, the term *individualism* was coined in the early decades of the nineteenth century as a judgment against this new movement. In particular, it was employed as a term of disdain in opposition to the French Revolution and its noteworthy *Declaration of the Rights of Man* (1789). In its opening article, the declaration affirmed that all persons "are born and remain free and equal in rights. Social distinctions may be founded only upon the general good." It announced that the purpose of civil society is to preserve each individual's rights to "liberty, property, security, and resistance to oppression."

To Joseph de Maistre, a Catholic Restorationist, the first to employ the language of individualism, this revolution, with its declaration of the rights of the individual, constituted a frontal attack on the authority of the church and, in the fullness of its ramifications, would foment anarchy, resulting in the destruction of social order. It betokened a rejection of doctrinal tradition and undercut the control of spiritual and temporal offices. Individualism, in short, was anathema from the standpoint of the medieval ideal.

At about the same time, however, Claude Henri de Saint-Simon and his disciples also adopted the term *individualism* to criticize the French Revolution, but from a far more progressive angle. They, too, were concerned that an unmodified declaration of the rights of individuals would result in the fragmentation of the social order. However, over against the implied egoism of the French Revolution, they sought not to restore the medieval ideal, but to construct a new epoch of "universal association" imbued with a sense of moral responsibility, each person for all others. The Simonists designated this new political vision *socialism*.

Shortly thereafter, Robert Owen, a British industrialist, assumed a similar position, attacking the destructiveness of capitalist competition and promoting in its stead the creation of cooperative communities. The central fault of capitalist individualism was its failure to care for the welfare of the larger society (including the workers).

Despite these and other critical judgments, however, the spirit of individualism as the ideal of the modern world has steadily permeated the culture of the Western world, infusing virtually all arenas of its common life and radically affecting the ways we think and act. In turn, it has had widespread influence across the globe despite counter-movements of resistance. So modern philosophy, in its exploration of questions of truth, beauty, and goodness, turns for its evidence not to inherited wisdom but to reason and experience. Modern science, in its theories and hypotheses about the workings of the universe, relies on varying forms of experimentalism, not on traditional dogmas and speculations.

Modern politics, dismissing myths about the divine right of rulers, insists that the people are sovereign and therefore public opinion must be heeded in the formation of public policy. Modern economics resists all efforts at governmental or religious control of its mechanisms on the supposition that, accompanied by a rigorous set of rights to private property and free contracts, an open market is the most efficient way to operate the economy and expand the wealth of nations.

Modern religion has transformed faith from an objective institutional system, with imposed doctrines and rituals under the control of ecclesiastical authorities, into a matter of individual spiritual quest and personal decision, resulting over time in a fragmented array of denominational possibilities and spiritual pathways. Similarly, modern ethics has tended to turn aside from the concept of a universal moral order, with its contrary understanding that moral judgments are subjective and that individuals must determine their own values and goals to pursue.

Developments such as these throughout the West, epitomized with special vigor in the United States, are all expressive of the modern world view of individualism. They have, however, not prevailed without constant resistance from opposing cultural forces engaging diverse groups. Among those within North America we must count the cultures of indigenous peoples; Puritan communities in New England (and their successors); the plantation system in the southern states; the communalism of African American religious congregations; the occasional formation of communes (such as Robert Owen's New Harmony community); movements of working peoples, democratic socialists, feminists and womanists, and different strains of Christianity (evangelical Protestants, mainstream Protestants, Roman Catholics). Yet over against such forces of resistance, the spirit of individualism has endured in its dominance in modern Western culture—with its genius, yet also with its inversion, an inversion that, as it plays out, belies its original impulse.

The original genius of individualism as a world view is its affirmation of the principle of human dignity—its deep respect for the worth of each individual person as a center of thought, feeling, and action.

The individualist version of the principle of human dignity is linked historically with the modern human rights movement, whose basic documents range from the American *Declaration of Independence* (1776) to and beyond the *Universal Declaration of Human Rights* (1948). Granting variations among modern proponents of human rights, they are joined in their effort to promote genuine respect for the individuality of each and every person on the supposition that one should have the freedom to think and to speak for oneself (autonomy); a space of one's own within which to act for oneself and by oneself (privacy); and the opportunities and facilities needed to develop one's own visions and dreams (empowerment). Autonomy, privacy, and empowerment are, in short, key requisites for the full recognition of individual human dignity. They are essential constituents of treating each person as a valued agent in the adventure of life.

While the principle of human dignity has roots in the historical beginnings of the West reaching back to ancient Israel, primitive Christianity, and classical Greek culture, it failed to be fully recognized or realized over subsequent centuries. Against that background the Enlightenment can be interpreted as a dramatic and welcome reappropriation of that principle.

However, we must note, that reappropriation was cast in a particular form that, ironically, has turned into its reversal as it became institutionalized. Modern individualism, that is, released energies that have, contrary to its own declarations of human rights, resulted in multiple kinds of domination and exploitation of individuals—particularly but not exclusively in the configurations and concentrations of political and economic power that have developed throughout the modern age.

Focusing on our own history as a case in point, we can recall that the United States, often considered to be a representative case of modern individualism par excellence, began, as its mythic history has it, in a search for personal freedom. It presumably created, in that process, a "new world." But in this land, that creation in actual fact entailed the near genocidal conquest of indigenous peoples—taking over their lands, almost obliterating the whole population, confining survivors to reservations. The enslavement of African peoples was condoned by the laws of the land. Women were prohibited from becoming full-fledged citizens.

As the development of the nation proceeded through its early decades, the imperialist ambitions of the new nation, dubbed "manifest destiny" by interpreters and advocates, while cloaked in the language of individual rights, contradicted the initial genius of the individualist principle with its conquests.

Moreover, in a dramatic turn initiated in the nineteenth century that radically altered the character of American culture, the transmutation of an agrarian social system of self-employed individuals (excluding, however, those noted above and others whose ethnic identity precluded full acceptance in the expanding nation) into a corporative economic system shaped by the impact of the industrial revolution and the expansion of modern technology resulted in a virtual inversion of the principle of individualism.

By the end of that century, most working peoples were in the employ of a corporate industry whose influence increasingly permeated all sectors of our common life and whose dominant concern was the "bottom line," not the principle of human rights. Within the work place, employees lost their presumed independence, subservient as they were to corporations for their livelihood. Even whole neighborhoods became dependent on decisions made in corporative board rooms in the interests not of the people but of the economic elite.

Throughout the twentieth century, corporativism has run through a number of phases, dominated currently by gigantic corporations that are transnational—highly diversified, given to merging, downsizing, outsourcing, changes in personnel and kind of activity—and driven by an impetus to compete in a global market and to do whatever is necessary to enhance corporate growth.

These corporations occupy a curious place in modern society. They are identified as belonging to the private sector. In what they do and how they act they are protected by principles of private property and free contract, thereby claiming to be treated legally as individuals. They resist efforts at regulation by public institutions, even as they are entangled in multiple ways with governmental and military operations to their benefit. They have struggled, with considerable success, to blunt efforts by the labor movement to enable working men and women to gain some control over conditions in the work place. In their defense, they tout the tradition of free enterprise and liberal democracy while their practices and effects belie the original intention of these modern institutional forms.

Since World War II they have been the primary impulse behind a process of economic globalization, extending their reach throughout the world, running roughshod over local cultures with their unique ways of life, impoverishing many peoples while creating new elites. Even within the United States, neighborhoods and communities, both rural and urban, have been profoundly transformed by the determinations—the comings and goings—of corporate powers driven not by decisions of citizens but by considerations, it is said, of economic necessity. Alliances forged among current forces of corporativism, nationalism, and militarism—despite tensions among their respective aims—have but reinforced the dramatic turn we have experienced over the past two centuries.

That turn toward a corporative society, in sum, is the perverse permutation of individualism as a way of life into its virtual antithesis. Defenders of the prevailing status of corporate America, nonetheless, constantly invoke the principle of individualism as a means of self-justification. Such an invocation, of course, is the strict meaning of ideology—the effort to make the interests of a dominant few appear to be the interests of all.

I do not mean through this indictment to imply that the common people in this land and elsewhere are wholly without the freedoms affirmed in modern declarations of human rights. Even under the most dire of conditions, the human spirit resists constraints and finds ways to express in word and action its yearnings and judgments, especially in the arts. Moreover, the modern human rights movement remains strong here and abroad in its resistance to egregious forms of oppression. Again, liberation movements of diverse groups over the decades (from minorities and workers, women and children, to gays and lesbians, prisoners and immigrants) have appealed to the tradition of human rights as an invaluable resource in their fight for freedom and equality.

Yet I would insist that there is a fundamental flaw in modern individualism that, given conditions within recent centuries, provided an opening for the tragic reversal to take place— a transmutation from the original vision of individualism into various kinds of domination and exploitation.

FROM INDIVIDUALISM TO SOLIDARITY

The fundamental flaw of modern individualism lies in the way it renders the self as an agent in the adventure of life. Its genius must be applauded, that is, its concentration on the unique creativity of the self and its effort to protect that central feature of our individuality, articulated so eloquently in the modern human rights movement. That is an essential dimension of our selfhood.

However, modern individualism is flawed in its neglect of a companion dimension of our selfhood—our intimate embeddedness in relationships with others. In its preeminent focus on individual creativity, it fails to acknowledge that the quality of our interactions with others is a necessary component of that creativity and of our personal identity. Given that flaw, it is unaware that we share a common destiny. It is blind to our two-sidedness: as creative agents and as social selves.

That is why I propose that, over against individualism, the language of solidarity is a way of synthesizing these interdependent dimensions of our selfhood.[6]

On the one hand, the principle of solidarity accepts the turn toward the subject brought to the fore by the Enlightenment, approving its rejection of the hierarchical and organic ideal of the medieval world. Each one of us should be respected and supported as a creative center of feeling, thought, and action.

Yet, while acknowledging our unique individuality, the principle of solidarity declares that we belong to one another within the immediate context of our lives. We inherit, for good or for ill, the opportunities and limitations of that context which forms the initial condition of our individual identity. At the same time, given that context, we bear responsibility for what we make of that moment—for how we reshape that beginning point in a form that both expresses our own unique sensibility and conduces to the flourishing of the entire community of life, including our selves.

Conjoining these dimensions of our selfhood, the principle of solidarity avoids the propensity of modern individualism toward egoism—by which I mean the pursuit of self-interest whether or not that pursuit redounds to the benefit or to the detriment of others. In its propensity toward egoism, modern individualism tends to render the surrounding world as instrumental to one's own self-defined good. One may, of course, befriend others or join in associated actions, but only as a matter of self-determination.

Among the tragic curiosities of modern individualism as it has played itself out over the decades is that, while in its beginnings it tended to promote personal egoism (I shall think and act as I will, in my own way and for my own goals), it has generated a history through which that principle has been (and still is) invoked to justify diverse forms of collective egoism with extensively destructive consequences.

As intimated above, a case in point is the impact of modern corporativism on our common life as it has developed since the closing decades of the nineteenth century. With this development, the right to private property, conceived originally as a necessary basis for a free citizenry, has been transformed into a principle defending corporate capitalism against regulation by governing agencies that were introduced originally to protect individuals and neighborhoods from harm and exploitation resulting from corporate action. Moreover, the development of corporate capitalism, combined with the progress of modern technology, has effected a radical transformation in the structure of American society from a community of independent property owners into a population of wage earners, dependent for their livelihood on complex hierarchical structures over which they exercise little control.

Again, modern corporations have become centers of concentrated political power, effecting a shift in the prevailing focus of public policy formation from human rights and the common good to the accumulation of wealth located predominantly in the hands of a small proportion of the population. In addition, through sophisticated techniques of advertising and marketing, corporations have managed, in large part, to transform our primary identity as active participants within the community to that of consumers whose happiness is linked to material acquisition and commercialized entertainment.

In all these respects, even in their acts of seeming benevolence, modern corporations are governed by an inner drive to expand, to beat out competitors, to gain ever greater control of the market, to bend alternative forces, political and social, toward their own ends. In sum, the modern corporation is an exemplary instance of collective egoism within the contemporary world, which, ironically, belies the originating impulse of the Enlightenment even as it claims principles of individualism as its justification.

In sharp contrast to the principle of modern individualism with its egoistic implications, I suggest that the covenantal tradition of ancient Judaism and primitive Christianity represents an early case of the principle of solidarity.[7] The central difference is that the covenantal world view at its best concentrates not exclusively on the personal agency and interests of the individual (or the collective acting as an individual) but on the quality of relations between and among selves within the community of life.

As represented in the classic narrative of the Exodus, the covenant at Sinai denotes a dramatic liberation from an oppressive social order (enslavement in the land of Egypt) and the creation of a radically new system of relations dedicated to the flourishing of the community as a whole through which the needs of each participant are fulfilled. Special provision is made for the most vulnerable—the widow, the fatherless, the stranger.

The precise configuration of each new covenant depicted in the scriptural texts varies according to its historical circumstances, but several qualities remain constant throughout them all. A covenantal community is characterized by its overarching concern to promote peace *(shalom)*, justice *(zedek)*, and loyalty *(hesed)*.

Peace, justice, and loyalty are relational qualities, specifying how the people are to live with one another throughout all their interactions—political, economic, and familial. They constitute moral responsibilities in the creation and sustenance of a holy commonwealth, embracing, in the final analysis, the entire community of life, however much its precise character may vary from region to region or from time to time.

These three qualities of interaction are mandated not as arbitrary commands from a higher authority, but as specifications of what it means to live a full and abundant life. While in the Hebraic narrative the emergence of a covenantal community is initiated by a call from the Lord God, its realization is contingent on the consent of the people with the realization that this kind of community is, in its effects, for their own good.

Within the Gospels of the early Christian movement, the character of the new covenant inaugurated at that time is summarized in Jesus' twofold commandment to love God and love the neighbor. This commandment integrates the qualities of peace, justice, and loyalty in a single adage. Love is not so much an individual feeling as a form for interaction directed toward the creation of a new world community of mutuality through which each participant may find fulfillment and joy.

The modern language of solidarity became widely used in the early decades of the nineteenth century, often among groups resisting the degrading social consequences of modern individualism. In such instances the appeal to solidarity signified a group of persons joined together in a common conviction that prevailing social conditions were the fundamental cause of widespread suffering and therefore in need of radical reconstruction to serve the general welfare. They were bonded in their sympathies with one another and in their purpose in advancing a way of life through which the community as a whole, including themselves, might benefit. In this sense it seems the modern appeal to solidarity is congruent with the covenantal tradition.

Relations infused with the character of solidarity are, according to some recent interpreters, akin to personal friendship and, more broadly, to the cultural practice of exchanging gifts where that practice represents the giving of self to self or group to group. Relations of friendship and gift exchange involve that kind of interaction in which the deepest joy is derived not from their utility to each individual participant separately (as in bargaining or market exchange), but from the relationship itself. In solidarity, the good is defined not merely as the attainment of what one wants for one's own pleasure but rather as the kind of symbiotic reciprocity through which, while diverse needs and pathways are honored, the good of the association itself, the common good, is especially cherished.

Sadly, appeals to covenantal solidarity have all too often been made to support exclusivist and conformist groups. Instances of such closed societies are ample, and their destructive effects are evident even in the history of the Hebrew people and the Christian tradition: tribalism, nationalism, racism, sexism, and anthropocentrism.

However, over against cases of closed societies, an impressive array of movements throughout human history has given voice to an inclusive understanding of solidarity as a moral necessity given the fundamentally interactive character of the adventure of life. These movements envision the need for a genuinely open society, acknowledging the constancy of change and the interconnective character of the unfolding universe.

Of the two ways of life I have placed under scrutiny—that of modern individualism and that of an inclusive solidarity—the latter is, I am persuaded, the more compelling for two fundamental reasons.

First, philosophically, it depicts more adequately our self-identity as creative agents within the context of an evolving community of life. We are not, most basically, separate and distinct individuals. We are not, that is, isolated beings, each one existing alone to follow our own singular yearning. Rather, we exist as individuals-in-community. We are participants in the continuing flow of the universe. In religious terms, we are co-workers in God's ongoing creation. As such, given our own creative capacities, we hold a responsibility in our interactions with other members of that creation to contribute to its advance into an open future. The language of solidarity as I intend it captures this way of understanding our status and our calling in the world.

Second, pragmatically, given our current historical circumstance with its particular challenges, the principle of solidarity provides a more promising way to move toward their effective resolution. The dominant problems of our age—environmental deterioration, persistent poverty, social divisiveness, devastating warfare—reach across all the boundaries we have constructed distinguishing diverse members of the community of life from one another. To approach these problems sensibly means we must negotiate with one another strategically and tactically. The resolution of such problems entails methods of reconciliation among opposing groups, including the redistribution of resources and the adoption of new ways of living together. Solidarity as a world view is far more encouraging as a beginning point in approaching these kinds of challenges than is individualism, with its tendency toward egoism and separatism.

At this time of historical crisis, the principle of solidarity directs us to the construction of a new world order—a world order characterized by a cooperative economy, participatory democracy, cultural diversity, gender equality, ecological sustenance, nonviolent means of conflict resolution, and global peace. The human rights movement generated with the emergence of modern individualism has an important place in such a new world, but with a change in focus and compass.

The function of the idea of human rights is, within this setting, not merely to protect individuals from undue interference by governments and other parties but to empower them to participate creatively within the ongoing community of life. For that purpose the idea of human rights must include economic and social rights, must recognize the rights of minority groups to sustain their own ways of living, and must be extended to embrace environmental sustainability.

In sum, the struggle between the world views of individualism and solidarity I discerned only dimly in my youth has reached a decisive point in history. While acknowledging the genius of the former in its initial impulse, we must now direct our energies toward the creation of a radically new way of living together so that all participants in the community of life might flourish. That has been the central vision of the covenantal tradition. That is the aspiration and commitment affirmed by the principle of solidarity.

NOTES

[1] Herbert Hoover, "New York City Speech," 1928, Herbert Hoover Library, Box 91. Available online.

[2] Herbert Hoover, *American Individualism* (Garden City, NJ: Doubleday, 1922).

[3] See George Lakoff, *Don't Think of an Elephant: Know Your Values and Frame the Debate* (White River Junction, VT: Chelsea Green Publishing, 2004).

[4] On the concept of individualism, see William Ernest Hocking, *The Lasting Elements of Individualism* (New Haven, CT: Yale University Press, 1937). A more recent analysis has been published by Steven Lukes in *Individualism* (Oxford: Basil Blackwell, 1973); and "(Types of) Individualism," *Dictionary of the History of Ideas* (2003), available online.

[5] Immanuel Kant, "What Is Enlightenment?" (1784), available online.

[6] On the meaning and pertinence of politics of solidarity in our times, see Douglas Sturm, *Solidarity and Suffering* (Albany, NY: SUNY Press, 1998).

[7] On the concept of the covenant throughout Jewish history and its impact on political development in the West, see the extensive work of Daniel Elazar. Pertinent chapters of his work available on the jcpa.org website include "The Covenant Tradition in Politics," "Covenant as a Political Concept," "Kinship and Consent," and "Authority, Power, and Leadership in the Jewish Polity."

16

May We Grow Together

Dolores R. Leckey

O God, the source of all life throughout the universe(s), known and unknown, we desire to live in the heart of your reality, not in our illusions. You who are creator of the truth, beauty, and goodness that give meaning to all our lives; you who chose to live among us and who continues to cast your lot with our struggles to live authentically; you whose spirit energizes us to participate fully in the communities of love that find diverse expression all through our world—how can we reflect the reality of your triune life?

Jesus gave us some clues. He said that you—creator, redeemer, spirit—count every hair on our heads. He told us that whenever a sparrow falls from the sky, you notice. And so too with human life. You value our individuality (even our quirkiness). When we notice the situation of others, especially different others, and act compassionately toward them, we are imaging your attentiveness and care.

We need to notice, too, how easily our individuality can harden into a rigid individualism. Then we fail to notice the sparrows, or we simply don't care. Soon we can fall into the trap of thinking that ultimate freedom is going it alone. That illusion drains the life from your world, and the real life from us, your people.

159

Help us, triune God, to understand that there is no life without relationship. Every life *begins* in relatedness, in an act of love. Every life grows in relatedness, first through the nourishment of mother to child, then through the widening circle of learning and discovery that moves through childhood and beyond, and finally, through our bodily return to earth in some fashion where we commingle with the primal elements of your creation.

Saint John of the Cross, the Carmelite mystic, said that in the evening of life only love matters. True. But it also matters every step of the way. We are born to love, not in the Hallmark romantic sense (though that is part of the mystery), but in the sturdy, real way of community, of ever-widening circles of community. It is this relationality that offers hope in the moments of decline in human civilization.

How can we realize more deeply this wonder, this mystery, this reflection of your divine life? Surely your word is a key. Your word alive in the Holy Scriptures, your word alive in the poet's imagination, your word alive in the richness of conversation, your word alive in sacraments that free us to be fully human and joined to one another, your word alive in prayer of all kinds. It is your word that strengthens us to resist the illusion of individualism while at the same time celebrating the individual reality of each person no matter the circumstances of his or her life.

As we strive to cherish the many manifestations of your word, may all *our* words be true ones. And may we continue to grow in the knowledge that *together* "we live and move and have our being" in you (Acts 17:28).

Amen.

PART 3
ORDINARY CHRISTIANS, EXTRAORDINARY HOPE

17

Thy Beloved Community Come

Deborah K. Blanks

O liberating and life-giving God, grant us the audacity of spirit and strength of mind to be your incarnate and living presence in the world.

You are nearer to us than the rhythmic beating of our hearts and much closer than either our hands or our feet. Before we have formed the words to speak or contemplated the thoughts that reveal the inner yearnings for your kingdom to come on earth even as it is in heaven—you hear us and you know us.

Your divine voice summons us in this *now moment* in history to be people of courage standing stalwartly against the principalities and powers. There are tremors of trouble that will not cease shaking the very foundations of our cosmic realm. There are seething tensions of racial unrest brooding in human hearts. There are spoken and unspoken cries for justice by countless members of the human family. There are suffering peoples everywhere and those who suffer for doing right. There are those who are victims of rampant, raging, and random violence in the cities of our nation. Yet the hunger for hope and longing for mercy stir within our souls.

O God, help us recognize our common humanity, armor us with your love, and cover us with your compassion. "You have no hands but our hands." Grant us the will to be the human lifeline that reaches beyond ourselves to redeem the life of another. "You have no feet but our feet." Grant us the courage to walk the pathway until the gateway of justice opens fully and all enter in. "You have no heart but our heart." Grant us the grace to live in such a way that thy beloved community come here on earth in our day, in our time—in this *now moment*. Amen.

Resisting the Powers of Death

A Sermon on Loving Life, Loving Justice

Christine M. Smith

Is such a fast that I choose,
   a day to humble oneself?
Is it to blow down the head like a bulrush,
   and to lie in sackcloth and ashes?
Will you call this a fast,
   a day acceptable to the LORD?

Is not this the fast that I choose:
   to loose the bonds of injustice,
   to undo the thongs of the yoke,
to let the oppressed go free,
   and to break every yoke?
Is it not to share your bread with the
      hungry,

I preached an earlier version of this sermon for the installation of Eldonna Hazen as pastor of First Congregational Church, United Church of Christ, Madison, Wisconsin, on February 11, 2007.

and bring the homeless poor into your
   house;
when you see the naked, to cover them,
and not to hide yourself from your own
   kin?
Then your light shall break forth like the
   dawn,
and your healing shall spring up quickly;
your vindicator shall go before you,
   the glory of the LORD shall be your rear
      guard.
Then you shall call, and the LORD will answer;
   you shall cry for help, and he will say,
      Here I am.
If you remove the yoke from among you,
   the pointing of the finger, the speaking of
      evil,
if you offer your food to the hungry
   and satisfy the needs of the afflicted,
then your light shall rise in the darkness
   and your gloom be like the noonday.
The LORD will guide you continually,
   and satisfy your needs in parched places,
   and make your bones strong;
and you shall be like a watered garden,
   like a spring of water,
   whose waters never fail.
Your ancient ruins shall be rebuilt;
   you shall raise up the foundations of
      many generations;
you shall be called the repairer of the
      breach,
   the restorer of streets to live in.

If you refrain from trampling the sabbath,
   from pursuing your own interests on my
      holy day;

if you call the sabbath a delight
   and the holy day of the LORD honorable;
if you honor it, not going your own ways,
      serving your own interests, or pursuing
         your own affairs,
then you shall take delight in the LORD,
      and I will make you ride upon the
         heights of the earth;
I will feed you with the heritage of your
      ancestor Jacob,
         for the mouth of the LORD has spoken.
         (Is 58:5–14)

Let us pray: O Holy One, open our hearts, our minds, and our spirits this day so that we might discern and hear the word we need to hear to live our lives faithfully and justly in your world. Amen.

The revolutionary Salvadoran poet Roque Dalton sings praises to life, love, and justice in his powerful resistance poem, "Like You."

Like you I
love love, life, the sweet smell
of things, the sky-blue
landscape of January days.

And my blood boils up
and I laugh through eyes
that have known the buds of tears.

I believe the world is beautiful
and that poetry, like bread, is for everyone.

And that my veins don't end in me
but in the unanimous blood
of those who struggle for life,

love,
little things,
landscape and bread,
the poetry of everyone.[1]

Here is a man in love with life. He is willing to drink it in, feel it, be moved by it, and express profound gratitude for it. His moving words become even more powerful when we recall that he was murdered in El Salvador when he was only forty years old, because he spent his life moving alongside those who struggle for love, landscape, bread, the poetry of everyone. Perhaps it is because he knew oppression and death firsthand, and was willing to face them and resist them, that he understood and felt such profound things about the power of life.

Eldonna and members and friends of this faith community, as I have reflected on your new journey together, I have thought of this poet who loves life and loves justice. I have thought of this faithful contemporary prophet who worked for life with such passion that his blood "boils up" and his eyes know "buds of tears." I have also been thinking about and hearing the voice of another visionary prophet, Isaiah. Both of these poets and prophets have been speaking to my heart and to my deepening understanding of the inseparable nature of resistance, justice, and hope.

Isaiah would be at home in this congregation. I think he would even stop to praise you for your many commitments to life and your many acts of faithfulness in our world. He would praise you, yes, but he would not stop there. It just isn't his way.

Instead, Isaiah would do what he always did so powerfully in his own day—he would speak a prophetic word to you. And he would challenge you to resist the powers of death even more because he was the kind of justice seeker, visionary voice, and agent of truth-telling and transformation that many of you seek to be. He longs for his beloved community of faith to resist the powers of death in ways that it has not yet imagined, and he confronts the people with what will be required of them if they are to be God's agents of justice and resistance:

> to loose the bonds of injustice
> to undo the thongs of the yoke
> to let the oppressed go free
>
> to share your bread with the hungry
> and bring the homeless poor into your
>   house;
> when you see the naked to cover them . . .
> and satisfy the needs of the afflicted.

Isaiah is speaking bold words here, horribly indicting words that are intended to remind his people that in the midst of injustice and oppression, and suffering and pain, bowing down one's head like a bulrush and lying in sackcloth and ashes is not enough to change the world. It is not that fasting is not holy and important; it is just that fasting is never enough. And so Isaiah reminds the members of his community that they must move their feet, their bodies, and their resources toward those who are most oppressed.

He calls his people back to the excruciatingly hard ministries that are theirs, and he is calling to us today to the ministries that are ours, the ministries that have been the calling of God's people throughout history. He is reminding us all that there is no separation between loving life, loving community, loving God, and loving justice. He joins Roque Dalton in affirming that the sweet smell of things and the sky-blue landscape of January days have everything to do with one's blood boiling over the reality of oppression and injustice and with struggling all one's days for the poetry of everyone. Poet and prophet alike remind us that while there is *any* form of oppression or disparity throughout all creation, we who believe in God cannot rest. *We must resist.*

All of us need to be reminded to resist the powers of death that are all around us, and yet as a community of faith you seem to know this truth about resistance in your hearts and souls already. You know what Christian dissent looks like in the real lives of people.

You know that the prison population has increased 300 percent in the last fifteen years, and your prison-ministry project is a tangible sign of compassion. Christian dissent!

You know that all children should have appropriate education and adequate health care, and your ministry with children in the Cherokee Heights Middle School is an embodied sign of presence and help. Christian dissent!

You know that lesbian, gay, bisexual, and transgendered people are still the targets of hatred and violence the world over, and your Rainbow People ministry is a bold sign of radical acceptance. Christian dissent!

You know that there are many people still living with HIV and AIDS who are isolated and judged, and your advocacy work on their behalf is a concrete expression of tender care. Christian dissent!

You know that there are people in Chiapas, Mexico, who are still struggling for their land and their lives, and your delegations to that place are a holy act of accompaniment and solidarity. Christian dissent![2]

You know that people need community in order to thrive and have the courage to do God's work in the world and that the idols of rugged individualism must be dismantled and the tender and strong bonds of community must be created. You proclaim in your bulletin that "all are welcome here." Christian dissent!

Do you know how incredibly faithful and brave your ministries are in a world filled with so little real community and so much violence, oppression, and hate; so much denial and turning away; so much silence about the things that are most important?

You understand with absolute clarity that tender and constant care of one another is essential. You strive to resist prejudice and hatred as you seek the just inclusion of all your members in the full life of this church. You know something profound about what it means to tend community as a radical act of resistance to the rampant individualism and social isolation in our day. And you know something holy about what it means to try to tend to the whole world as a radical act of resistance in a day when our nation is forever choosing acts of international intrusion and violence.

We need Christians like you as we begin to make our way through the twenty-first century—Christians who will love life, love justice, tend local communities of faith, and seek to tend the world as faithful global citizens. Christian dissent is about tending community, and it is surely about tending the world.

When I think about the importance of *tending community*, and loving one another deeply and tenderly, I remember an early experience in my ministry. I was a pastor at Epworth United Methodist Church in Columbus, Ohio, and one of the members of the church asked me to pay a call on a young couple. They had just experienced the birth of their second child, and there were complications, lots of horrible complications. I made my way to the hospital to meet them for the first time, and to baptize their tiny newborn baby. It was a terrible time. It was an absolutely holy time.

They were a young couple, with no church home to call their own, and their baby was very, very sick. After her baptism, she lingered between life and death for a few weeks. This young, grief-stricken couple started coming to church, and they never missed a Sunday after that day in the hospital. Our faith community came to know them, and reach out to them, and draw them into a sustaining circle of love and care.

The days brought one painful decision after another, and their baby finally died. We spent hours together planning the memorial service and crying at their kitchen table. Many people cried around their kitchen table. There were "buds of tears" surrounding them for weeks. The Epworth community members knew for a fact that their veins did not end in themselves but in the "unanimous blood" of all those who struggle for life. And when it was time to say our goodbyes to this child, the whole community of Epworth Church gathered in circled chairs around this young couple as we told story after story of moments of unexpected joy, of pain, of tender support, and of agonizing loss.

This was the church at its finest. Here was a community of people who knew how to resist the impulse to flee, to isolate themselves, socially and religiously, from those in pain. And Isaiah's promise was so true, for God satisfied our needs in a parched place that seemed unbearable, made our bones strong enough to endure what seemed so crushing, and enabled our community to be like a spring whose waters never failed.

With this experience in mind and on this special day, I pray for you, First Congregational Church. I pray that you will continue to enable each other to have the tenderness and courage it takes to fold your arms around the wounded in hospital rooms, at kitchen tables, and beside people's sick pets. I pray that you will continue to pour yourselves into every empty heart during rituals of healing, through those hard moments when people lose their jobs, and in the midst of broken dreams and long months of grieving. I pray that you will cry out for hidden sorrows in your midst, for the gay father who has lost his children, for the teenage girl who is quietly starving herself to death, for the woman who is beaten in her own home.

Your tears and your arms of comfort and support may be the living embodiment of God's tender, saving care. And if you resist the powers of death that are at the heart of rugged individualism and continue to embrace the life of community, you shall be called "the repairer of the breach, the restorer of streets to live in" (Is 58:12).

But the voice of Roque Dalton and the challenges of Isaiah will not let us rest here. Compassion and tenderness within our faith community are precious things, even though difficult to embody with constancy and care, and yet Isaiah calls us into the larger world, far beyond our life together, and into a relationship with the most oppressed and marginalized. He invites us to love life, and to love justice, and to stretch out our veins way beyond this place.

When I think about the radicality of *tending the world,* I don't have to think long before my whole being is transported back to Guatemala. Perhaps many of you know that within the past two years I have had the great blessing of traveling to Guatemala on two occasions with students and friends of United Theological Seminary of the Twin Cities, including Eldonna and her partner Cathy. On both trips we went to Guatemala to try to move our very privileged lives just a bit closer to the lives of indigenous Mayan people, who are oppressed in ways many of us cannot imagine.

Guatemala is a country filled with indigenous Mayan women and men forgotten by the world. It is a country where the grinding genocide and massive violence from the Spanish conquest reverberate until this day, and where there is stunning beauty and horrifying trauma from a thirty-six-year-old civil war prompted by our government's interference. Guatemala is also a country filled with acts of hope, tenacious resistance, and so much life. Day after day I witnessed individuals and whole communities relentlessly trying to embody Isaiah's passionate pleas:

> to loose the bonds of injustice,
> to undo the thongs of the yoke,
> to let the oppressed go free,
> and to break every yoke?
> Is it not to share your bread with the
> hungry,

and bring the homeless poor into your
    house;
when you see the naked, to cover them,
and not to hide yourself from your own
    kin?
Then your light shall break forth like the
    dawn,
and your healing shall spring up quickly.
    (Is 58:6–8)

I see Carmen, who has lived in the barrio of La Esperanza for twenty-three years. I see her blood boiling up through laughter and tears as she works steadily for the employment of women and for the dignity of girls. I see the women she works with striving to mobilize and inspire a whole community in its struggle for justice, for water, for day care, for education, and for basic, life-giving health care. I can hear her saying,

"My veins don't end in me
but in the unanimous blood
of those who struggle for life,
love,
little things,
landscape and bread,
the poetry of everyone."

Carmen and so many others in this poor barrio are resisting the powers of death. They are tending community, and they are tending the world.

I hear the voice of Calixta, a Mayan holy woman committed to the preservation of Mayan ritual and culture, saying, as she leaves us, "Just remember that while you are thinking, people are dying." Her veins are the veins of people everywhere resisting the injustices of cultural and religious oppression. Calixta is resisting the powers of death. She is tending community, and she is tending the world.

I hear Pastor Diego, who lived through the death of half of his congregation during the civil war in the 1980s, talk about the Central American Free Trade Agreement (CAFTA) and what must be done if the indigenous widows' cooperative in Chontala is to survive. "The river is coming, like the Rio Grande," he says. "We cannot stop the river, so it is good to teach poor people how to survive in the river." His veins are forever and eternally tied to the veins of these widows he pastors, and to the project they have created together to change their lives and the lives and futures of their children. Pastor Diego and all the widows of Chontala are resisting the powers of death. They are tending community, and they are tending the world.

I see Blanca's tears and hear her voice as she describes the work of the families of the detained and disappeared—their fourteen-year effort to find clandestine graves and exhume the bones of her son and thousands of others so that they might have a dignified burial. "Our sons and daughters had different visions of a new life," she says. Digging in the earth of mass graves, she chooses to connect her veins to all those men, women, and children who have disappeared and been murdered, and to all those family members who still await some closure to the horror. Blanca and all her *companeras* and *companeros* are resisting the powers of death. They are tending community, and they are tending the world.

I hear the soft and life-long committed voice of Sister Ana Marie Noth. She declares with absolute resolve that those who have suffered so much violence must be cared for holistically, with herbs and healing touch, with nutritional guidance and gentle massage, with conversation and loving presence. Her life of faithful solidarity has mingled her veins with the veins of the indigenous people of Guatemala in ways that might teach all of us what "unanimous blood" can mean. On the walls of the healing center she has founded, these words appear: *No conozco la palabra imposible* (I do not know the word *impossible*). She and those she works with at the healing center are resisting the powers of death. They are tending community, and they are tending the world.[3]

"To loose the bonds of injustice, to undo the thongs of the yoke, and to let the oppressed go free" means that we must resist the great powers of death and take a stand for life with our words, our lives, and our embodied acts. We are called to resist together all the violent crucifixions that still abound. We are called to tend community, and we are called to tend the world. Christian dissent!

Breaking yokes and setting the oppressed free is about knowing with certainty that your veins do not stop with you but mingle with the unanimous blood of all who struggle for life. It is about loving life and loving justice.

I pray for you, Eldonna and First Congregational Church. I pray that whatever you do or wherever you go on this new journey together, you will continue to love life and love justice, that you will tend your own community and continue to tend the world. That you will let your blood boil up at times, and that you will keep resisting all the powers of death around you. That you will take action against the abuse of children's bodies and against the marginalization of our elders. That you will urge every religious community to build ramps, hire sign-language interpreters, and work tirelessly to dismantle the violence of white racism. That you will raise your religious voices against dying farm workers. That you will advocate for the civil rights of lesbian, gay, bisexual, and transgendered people. That you will work to change this country's economic policies, which continue to kill the indigenous people of Guatemala and Chiapas and millions of other peoples the world over.

If you embody this kind of resistance, this kind of transformation, and if you love life and love justice this passionately, your light shall break forth like the dawn, and you shall remove the yoke from among you (Is 58:8–9).

Step to your calling gladly, each one of you and all together. Tend your own community, and tend the world. The

heights of the earth await you, and may the grace and power
of God be with you.

Amen!

NOTES

[1] Roque Dalton, "Like You"/"Como Tu," in *Clandestine Poems/
Poemas Cladestinos* (Willimantic, CT: Curbstone Press, 1990), 39,
reprinted with permission of Curbstone Press (www.curbstone.org).
Distributed by Consortium.

[2] Information about First Congregational Church's ministries can
be found on the firstcongmadison.org website.

[3] Each time I have gone to Guatemala or to Chiapas, Mexico,
with a delegation of people, the women and men there have encouraged all of us to share their life stories when we return home. I have
used all of the names mentioned in this part of the sermon with
permission.

Hope for Tomorrow

Dwight N. Hopkins

O God, you have been so good to us. In the dangers and unforeseen twists and turns of life, you have continually made a way out of no way. We have been blessed by your mercy and your grace to perform practices of justice toward our neighbors that we often find not humanly possible. We have been just as blessed to discover that we humans, in our diversity, tragedy, and heroic efforts, are empowered by your energy to still love one another in the midst of pressures of daily living. The world is still here. Human community is still here. And we are still here.

O God, you have chosen to be with us inside of us, empowering us to battle the material demons and spiritual principalities and powers that awake at the midnight hour in our lives. Each of us stands grateful for the times you show up to help us remove the overcast terror of the unknown. Especially when the murkiness of our prophetic horizon waivers in the face of the Evil One, you rouse our inner good selves with the passion to hope and the joy to see and to live the best of life, in spite of it all. You even carry us as on eagle wings in the subconscious moments of our sleep. Because of your love and power to empower us, we awake from the depths of slumber and exit from the trials of the overcast experiences to walk into the sunrise of joy in the morning.

O God, it is because of who you are and your mercy that we are able to draw on the best of what it means to be an individual self in relation to our neighbor, even those we disagree with. Because of who you are—God all by yourself—we know that there is a possibility of "taking a crooked stick and hitting a straight lick." The miracle of the human condition is that we can confront an ordinary situation and produce extraordinary results. Is this not what it means to live in community with nature, the four-legged creatures, the winged ones of the air, and the dwellers in the sea? Though the worst of the human predicament pressures us to cut short the life of creation, still people move forward in search of the right balance between humanity and nature.

O God, you have taught us about and shown us your global concern for and love of all communities across this world. Here ethnic differences, religious practices, and ritual performances show forth as the rainbow beauty that results from the sunshine of your imagination. In the diversities of the world, your strength is a rock of salvation to hold the many together as one earthly family. And as we struggle human group against human group over petty priorities and foolish futilities, every now and then, some of us, with childlike innocence, see that we are all made in the image of God.

O God, most decisively for us Christians, it is the carpenter of Nazareth who walked this earth over two thousand years ago and proclaimed the good news for the materially poor, the spiritually wounded, and the lonely outcasts. Because God chose to reveal Godself in the messiness of biological life and in the ambiguity of human culture, we know in this revelation of spirit in the flesh of Jesus how we humans, too, can be co-walker, co-talker, and co-server with the least of these. And so to live with the fullness of joy for the immediate now and the hope of tomorrow, we lean on God's unchanging hands. This revelation two millennia ago offered humanity the way to endless possibilities of being fully human in service to the "other." This is the ultimate happiness of the now. In fact, in a profound sense, what Jesus taught us is that heaven is knowing the purpose of our existence—to be healed individuals in service to those least off. With the life of that historical One who still accompanies us as today's One, all of creation can breathe together into the promise of the future One. Amen.